LB
2341
M277
1983

S0-EDQ-455

Management Techniques for Small and Specialized Institutions

Andrew J. Falender, John C. Merson, *Editors*

NEW DIRECTIONS FOR HIGHER EDUCATION
MARTIN KRAMER, *Editor-in-Chief*

Number 42, June 1983

Paperback sourcebooks in
The Jossey-Bass Higher Education Series

Jossey-Bass Inc., Publishers
San Francisco • Washington • London

Andrew J. Falender, John C. Merson (Eds.).
Management Techniques for Small and Specialized Institutions.
New Directions for Higher Education, no. 42.
Volume XI, number 2.
San Francisco: Jossey-Bass, 1983.

New Directions for Higher Education Series
Martin Kramer, *Editor-in-Chief*

Copyright © 1983 by Jossey-Bass Inc., Publishers
and
Jossey-Bass Limited

Copyright under International, Pan American, and Universal
Copyright Conventions. All rights reserved. No part of
this issue may be reproduced in any form—except for brief
quotation (not to exceed 500 words) in a review or professional
work—without permission in writing from the publishers.

New Directions for Higher Education (publication number USPS
990-880) is published quarterly by Jossey-Bass Inc., Publishers.
New Directions is numbered sequentially—please order extra
copies by sequential number. The volume and issue numbers
above are included for the convenience of libraries. Second-class
postage rates paid at San Francisco, California, and at
additional mailing offices.

Correspondence:
Subscriptions, single-issue orders, change of address notices,
undelivered copies, and other correspondence should be sent to
New Directions Subscriptions, Jossey-Bass Inc., Publishers,
433 California Street, San Francisco, California 94104.

Editorial correspondence should be sent to the Consulting Editor,
Martin Kramer, 2807 Shasta Road, Berkeley, California 94708.

Library of Congress Catalogue Card Number LC 82-84189

International Standard Serial Number ISSN 0271-0560

International Standard Book Number ISBN 87589-952-8

Cover art by Willi Baum

Manufactured in the United States of America

Ordering Information

The paperback sourcebooks listed below are published quarterly and can be ordered either by subscription or as single copies.

Subscriptions cost $35.00 per year for institutions, agencies, and libraries. Individuals can subscribe at the special rate of $21.00 per year *if payment is by personal check.* (Note that the full rate of $35.00 applies if payment is by institutional check, even if the subscription is designated for an individual.) Standing orders are accepted.

Single copies are available at $7.95 when payment accompanies order, and *all single-copy orders under $25.00 must include payment.* (California, Washington, D.C., New Jersey, and New York residents please include appropriate sales tax.) For billed orders, cost per copy is $7.95 plus postage and handling. (Prices subject to change without notice.)

To ensure correct and prompt delivery, all orders must give either the *name of an individual* or an *official purchase order number.* Please submit your order as follows:

Subscriptions: specify series and subscription year.
Single Copies: specify sourcebook code and issue number (such as, HE8).

Mail orders for United States and Possessions, Latin America, Canada, Japan, Australia, and New Zealand to:
    Jossey-Bass Inc., Publishers
    433 California Street
    San Francisco, California 94104

Mail orders for all other parts of the world to:
    Jossey-Bass Limited
    28 Banner Street
    London EC1Y 8QE

New Directions for Higher Education Series
Martin Kramer, *Editor-in-Chief*

HE1   *Facilitating Faculty Development,* Mervin Freedman
HE2   *Strategies for Budgeting,* George Kaludis
HE3   *Services for Students,* Joseph Katz
HE4   *Evaluating Learning and Teaching,* C. Robert Pace
HE5   *Encountering the Unionized University,* Jack II. Schuster
HE6   *Implementing Field Experience Education,* John Duley
HE7   *Avoiding Conflict in Faculty Personnel Practices,* Richard Peairs
HE8   *Improving Statewide Planning,* James L. Wattenbarger, Louis W. Bender
HE9   *Planning the Future of the Undergraduate College,* Donald G. Trites
HE10 *Individualizing Education by Learning Contracts,* Neal R. Berte
HE11 *Meeting Women's New Educational Needs,* Clare Rose
HE12 *Strategies for Significant Survival,* Clifford T. Stewart, Thomas R. Harvey
HE13 *Promoting Consumer Protection for Students,* Joan S. Stark

HE14 *Expanding Recurrent and Nonformal Education,* David Harman
HE15 *A Comprehensive Approach to Institutional Development,* William Bergquist,
   William Shoemaker
HE16 *Improving Educational Outcomes,* Oscar Lenning
HE17 *Renewing and Evaluating Teaching,* John A. Centra
HE18 *Redefining Service, Research, and Teaching,* Warren Bryan Martin
HE19 *Managing Turbulence and Change,* John D. Millett
HE20 *Increasing Basic Skills by Developmental Studies,* John E. Roueche
HE21 *Marketing Higher Education,* David W. Barton, Jr.
HE22 *Developing and Evaluating Administrative Leadership,* Charles F. Fisher
HE23 *Admitting and Assisting Students after* Bakke, Alexander W. Astin, Bruce Fuller,
   Kenneth C. Green
HE24 *Institutional Renewal Through the Improvement of Teaching,* Jerry G. Gaff
HE25 *Assuring Access for the Handicapped,* Martha Ross Redden
HE26 *Assessing Financial Health,* Carol Frances, Sharon L. Coldren
HE27 *Building Bridges to the Public,* Louis T. Benezet, Frances W. Magnusson
HE28 *Preparing for the New Decade,* Larry W. Jones, Franz A. Nowotny
HE29 *Educating Learners of All Ages,* Elinor Greenberg, Kathleen M. O'Donnell,
   William Bergquist
HE30 *Managing Facilities More Effectively,* Harvey H. Kaiser
HE31 *Rethinking College Responsibilities for Values,* Mary Louise McBee
HE32 *Resolving Conflict in Higher Education,* Jane E. McCarthy
HE33 *Professional Ethics in University Administration,* Ronald H. Stein,
   M. Carlota Baca
HE34 *New Approaches to Energy Conservation,* Sidney G. Tickton
HE35 *Management Science Applications to Academic Administration,* James A. Wilson
HE36 *Academic Leaders as Managers,* Robert H. Atwell, Madeleine F. Green
HE37 *Designing Academic Program Reviews,* Richard F. Wilson
HE38 *Successful Responses to Financial Difficulties,* Carol Frances
HE39 *Priorities for Academic Libraries,* Thomas J. Galvin, Beverly P. Lynch
HE40 *Meeting Student Aid Needs in a Period of Retrenchment,* Martin Kramer
HE41 *Issues in Faculty Personnel Policies,* Jon W. Fuller

Contents

Editors' Notes   **1**
Andrew J. Falender, John C. Merson

Chapter 1. Strategic and Financial Planning   **5**
John C. Merson

College administrators need a management process that continually renews the institution's sense of direction while ensuring that plans are matched to available resources.

Chapter 2. The Presidency of a Small College   **11**
Dan C. West

The responsibilities of a college president range from the board of trustees to faculty and curriculum. Knowing when to accept the presidency, what to do while there, and when to leave are important aspects of the job.

Chapter 3. Some Notes on Fund Raising   **25**
Robert J. Corcoran

The key elements of a capital campaign must be in place long before the campaign is launched; indeed, the public phase shold be viewed as the final phase of a long process.

Chapter 4. Student Recruitment and Admissions   **33**
Carl Allen

There are two keys to effective student recruitment: creativity in seeking applicants and mobilization of institutional support for the admission program.

Chapter 5. The Public Image of a Small College   **41**
Rosemary Ashby

The author describes a five-year effort to project a new and more realistic public image to bring about improvements in student recruitment and fund raising.

Chapter 6. Searching for Senior Administrators   **49**
James M. Unglaube

College trustees and other members of search committees can take steps to improve the likelihood that senior vacancies will be filled on time, within budget, and without unpleasant surprises.

Chapter 7. Organizing and Staffing a Small College   **59**
Adele Simmons

Managing effectively with limited resources requires senior staff members to assume a variety of tasks. Bright young administrators can develop their skills while covering key functions.

Chapter 8. Computer-Supported Information Systems   65
William H. Mayhew

The author describes the planning and implementation of a computerized information system at a fictional but representative small college.

Chapter 9. Providing Focus for Financial Management   73
Andrew J. Falender

This case study of a financial turnaround describes strategies that can balance costs and resources.

Chapter 10. Small Colleges and Associations   85
Frank A. Tredinnick, Jr.

Associations can provide information and expertise that individual institutions do not always possess.

Chapter 11. The Board of Trustees   91
Robert L. Qualls

Building an effective board requires attention to trustees' roles and responsibilities, selection of new trustees, board organization, and criteria for measuring trustees' performance.

Index   97

Editors' Notes

In any size or type of institution, the senior administrator manages the process of obtaining resources and using them to meet organizational objectives. In some respects, managing in a small institution is similar to the managing process in a large organization. In other, significant respects, it is not.

In large and small institutions alike, the manager must define institutional objectives and determine how to reach them. Many large institutions pursue a broad range of competing objectives. Different though they may be one from another, all small colleges share one trait: They focus on relatively few objectives while trying to develop programs that support multiple objectives. Obviously, even the very large institution will be threatened in the long run by the absence of a coherent strategy. However, in the small colleges, and especially in the specialized institutions, the uniqueness of their objectives or niche in the education market is the key to their existence. Deviation from a well-defined strategy may result in a crippling loss of momentum, even in the short run.

The small institution experiences a thinner margin of safety than its larger counterpart—lower financial reserves, greater sensitivity to declining enrollment, proportionately higher fixed costs, fewer opportunities for new or expanded sources of income, and fewer opportunities for financial retrenchment. The result is that managerial mistakes are much more serious in the small institution. Losing sight of the institution's objective is just one of many fatal errors that the manager can make.

The unique managerial needs of a small institution must also be recognized. The importance of functional expertise is equalled by the requirement that administrators must be able to focus directly on the institution's objectives. Administrators must also be able to manage a wide range of responsibilities. The head of a small fund-raising office requires a far broader range of talents than the director of a large office does. The president of a college with a small development staff must be more actively involved in alumni and public relations than the president of an institution that has a large development office.

At the same time, the lessons that individuals in small institutions have learned can be useful to large organizations. The breadth of experience that a manager acquires in a small college provides excellent training for managing a larger operation. The affiliated institutes and independent departments of large universities are in many ways similar to small colleges. The reader of the chapters in this sourcebook will perceive many instances in which the author's views are applicable to large institutions.

We begin with John Merson's chapter on strategic and financial planning, since we consider these tasks a logical starting point for any senior manager in a small institution. This first step can be difficult for the chief executive of the small college, since "fighting fires" and the "overflowing in-box" will always seem more pressing than planning, especially when the president must function as the institution's chief planning officer. The planning approach suggested in Chapter One focuses on key issues, avoids lengthy reports, and gives high priority to financial constraints. Use of a personal computer to support and speed the consideration of options is advocated.

In Chapter Two, Dan West provides an overview of the management process in a small institution. He emphasizes the importance of fund raising and admissions responsibilities. West, who has been president of Arkansas College since 1972, tends to place the highest priority on the president's fund-raising efforts. In Chapter Three, fund-raising consultant Robert Corcoran describes effective techniques for small-college capital campaigns. His recommendations are based on his analysis of the most promising sources of support for small colleges. In Chapter Four, Carl Allen discusses the implications of the dwindling pool of college applicants. He predicts that admissions will begin to be accorded high priority by college presidents. Finally, in Chapter Five, Rosemary Ashby looks at the recent history of her institution to note the impact of public image on fund raising and admissions. She describes how an institution's public image can be improved.

The administration of a small college includes finding the right people, assigning responsibilities to them, and guiding their efforts so that they work toward the organization's mission as efficiently as possible. These topics are treated in Chapters Six through Eleven. In Chapter Six, James Unglaube discusses the administrative search process. He focuses on systematically organized searches for presidents and vice-presidents. In Chapter Seven, Adele Simmons covers the organization of administrative personnel. She recommends against attempts to find the ideal structure. Instead, she advocates a flexible set of arrangements under which frequent shifts in assignments can occur. She also describes how people at all levels have to be willing to take on a variety of tasks so that key functions can be covered, especially when the president's role requires frequent absences from campus.

Good information flow is as necessary in small institutions as it is in large institutions. In Chapter Eight, William Mayhew explains that computerized information systems can be flexible without being expensive. He surveys the lengthy developmental process of information systems and concludes that innovative risk takers may have better opportunities in small institutions than they do in large ones. In Chapter Nine, Andrew Falender argues that efforts to minimize expenses and maximize revenues have little value unless they also meet institutional objectives. He explains why top-rate financial plans have little effect unless they are designed with a view toward successful implementation.

The concern of small colleges with making good use of scarce resources leads Frank A. Tredinnick to look in Chapter Ten at ways of using association memberships to advantage. The manager in a small college must constantly find ways of obtaining services that supplement internal capabilities. Just as the institution's information systems can be developed without purchasing an in-house computer, association memberships can be used to strengthen federal and state relations without adding full-time staff positions in these areas. Finally, in Chapter Eleven, Robert L. Qualls discusses the issues that small colleges face in recruiting, organizing, and retaining trustees. Board support for institutional progress can be strengthened by keeping trusteeship a vital and active role.

Among the many lessons that we have learned in assembling these chapters is that academic managers, unlike their teaching and research-oriented colleagues, have little time for writing, especially in small institutions where managers must handle many jobs at once. Thus, we are very grateful to the authors for taking time to write about the challenges and opportunities that they face.

Andrew J. Falender
John C. Merson
Editors

Andrew J. Falender is chief executive officer of the New England Conservatory of Music. Before coming to Boston in 1975, he was an assistant director of the National Institute of Education.

John C. Merson, a former Woodrow Wilson Foundation administrative intern and management consultant to colleges, is vice-president for marketing with The Computer Factory, Inc., a public company engaged in the sale and service of personal computers.

*How do you keep the planning process simple and issue-driven
so that the workload is manageable and the results are useful?*

Strategic and Financial Planning

John C. Merson

"I know that our institution needs a comprehensive strategic plan, but things
are changing so fast I can't get the time for senior managers to work together
in producing one. Besides, it would be obsolete as soon as we finished it."
Undoubtedly, these words are familiar. Administrators agree that plans are
needed, but most administrators also believe that a strategic plan worthy of the
name would not only take too much time and staff effort to develop, it would
also be hard to change, and it would be too vague to provide a useful guide for
day-to-day operations. This chapter describes a process that is relatively simple to carry out, that is easy to modify at regular intervals, and that can be
converted into specific financial plans. It also covers the use of personal computers in making operational and financial planning more accessible to administrators and easier to analyze and modify.

Strategic Planning

An annual cycle that relates reporting, analysis, and planning steps
provides the best framework for strategic planning. Monthly meetings to discuss staff reports and proposals on plans, budgets, and results can ensure that
four key stages are covered: evaluation (analysis of past results and current
programs and support services), planning (renewal and possible revision of
mission, long-term goals, and strategies), resource allocation (selection of
near-term objectives and action plans), and financial planning (conversion of
action plans into financial forecasts and budgets).

A. J. Falender and J. C. Merson (Eds.). *Management Techniques for Small and Specialized Institutions.*
New Directions for Higher Education, no. 42. San Francisco: Jossey-Bass, June 1983.

Evaluation. The first stage of the planning process focuses on the organization's recent past as well as on its present and future. Managers prepare brief summaries of program results in relation to the objectives that were set for the programs. The institution takes stock both of its overall health and of the major programs in which it invests the bulk of its resources. Issues currently facing the institution are identified, and future problems are anticipated on the basis of present trends. All these issues become the agenda for the planning efforts that occur during the next three stages. A brief staff report summarizes these issues and describes the planning agenda.

Planning. In the second stage, managers review the institution's mission statement and the general goals that have been articulated for the institution. Statements of mission and goals are relatively durable, and probably require only minor changes from one year to the next. Thus, this stage places the emphasis on appraising the strategic approaches that have explicitly or implicitly been chosen as the means for realizing these goals.

For example, suppose that one goal is to provide students with a liberal education. One strategic approach to reaching this goal emphasizes attracting students who are strongly committed to a broad-based exposure to the humanities and sciences. These students would spend the better part of their first two years taking courses outside the major disciplines taught by teams of senior faculty members with an interdisciplinary perspective. Only as juniors would students select a major field and begin to concentrate or prepare for graduate and professional studies. This approach would not work for an institution where most entering students lacked a commitment to liberal education, that is, for an institution that enrolled many first-generation college students and students whose primary concern is completing vocational preparation by the end of their undergraduate career. At such institutions, the most effective strategic approach might be to infuse a liberal education perspective into the course requirements for each major so that students would be able to begin vocational studies without sacrificing their general education needs. To take an example from the area of student services, suppose that one goal of the institution is to provide students with a high degree of computer literacy. One strategic approach might be to offer courses—optional or required—that expose students to the major potential uses of computers in the worlds of work and education. Another approach would be to facilitate computer applications within the framework of a broad range of existing courses and extracurricular activities.

The end product of this second stage is a brief report redefining or restating the institution's mission, goals, and strategies. The report should be approved by the board of trustees, it should be circulated widely among administration and faculty. Just as important as developing an institutional sense of direction is ensuring that it is widely and deeply shared.

Resource Allocation. The third stage of the strategic planning process is aimed at selecting a small number of programs—no more than ten—that are vital to achieving the organization's goals. Senior managers can make these choices working together as a group. Each program chosen will then receive priority attention. For these programs, energy will be focused on setting objectives, developing action plans, and supporting the plans with resource levels adequate to ensure the achievement of proposed objectives.

It seems to be widely assumed that all education and support programs should receive equal attention. However, all programs are not equally important to the institution's effectiveness. Indeed, many if not most programs can continue unchanged in scope, thrust, and funding from one year to the next. Thus, planning efforts should be concentrated at the margins, that is, on programs with great unrealized potential, on programs that face serious problems, on programs that are ready to be phased out or eliminated, and on programs that are experiencing substantial growth in size or complexity. The focused approach enables senior managers to dedicate their limited time and effort to program areas in which major investment or disinvestment decisions must be made.

The resource allocation stage culminates in the specification of action plans for each major program. These action plans should cover a period of at least three years. Where capital construction is involved, the time horizon should be longer. However, not all program plans need to cover the same time period or to provide the same level of detail. The next year or two should be described in more detail than the years beyond. At the end of this stage, a brief staff report is prepared for review and action by the trustees. Following board approval, with such modifications as are needed, the report is circulated among senior managers and faculty department heads. Here again, as in the preceding stage, the aim is to promote understanding and support of the plan's principal elements.

Financial Planning. The fourth and last stage of the process is directed at converting action plans into financial plans. This stage has three steps. The first step is to forecast trends in costs and resources for areas not affected by the plan. These areas can include some education and support programs. The second step is to forecast operational and financial variables that are relatively stable or predictable. These variables can include endowment income, certain categories of gift and grant support, and major maintenance expenditures. The third and final step focuses on areas in which significant changes are planned or anticipated. Some of these changes are totally or primarily beyond the institution's control. For example, employee benefit and utility costs are difficult both to predict and to control. Other changes, such as in tuition fees, can be controlled, but it is hard to forecast their effect on enrollment. Hence, tuition increases can be considered feasible only within a narrow range. In still other areas, such as student financial aid, there are complex, interdependent relationships among tuition, institutional aid policies, and federal and state funding levels.

Colleges can use simulation models to deal systematically with such interrelationships. A model that simulates the interaction of many operational and financial variables can illustrate the outcome of many different planning scenarios. Such what-if analysis is valuable not only in selecting viable strategies for further consideration but also in ruling out options that are financially or otherwise unrealistic. However, the ultimate choice between one strategy and another or between one combination of plans and another generally has less to do with matters of finance than it does with the manager's personal attitudes toward risk and change. Nevertheless, financial feasibility tests can still be applied in making an initial selection from a wide range of choices. Personal computers can provide useful support in financial planning. Use of computers for this purpose is discussed in the final section of this chapter.

Organizing the Process

The chief executive officer (CEO) of the institution should assume responsibility for directing the planning process and be personally involved in all phases of the work. This approach reinforces the importance of planning as a routine aspect of every administrator's job and encourages every manager to devote an adequate share of his or her time to planning.

Small colleges are generally quite lean in their administrative structures, and the number of staff positions available to support planning as an organization-wide process is severely limited. For these reasons, it is unwise to establish a separate planning office in a small college unless the unit is placed under the CEO's direction and unless it also performs other related administrative functions, such as institutional research or development support.

The CEO should guide the planning process by convening regular meetings of the senior administrative team. Monthly meetings generally serve to keep planning issues in sharp focus and avoid shifting too much of the planning effort into the budget-preparation cycle. While each administrator is responsible for proposing goals, strategies, and action plans for his or her areas of responsibility, group meetings allow for coordination and teamwork on issues that cut across individual role assignments.

The planning process should be carried out as an annual cycle; it should be carefully integrated with other key administrative functions. While no single timetable will work equally well for all colleges, the schedule displayed in Figure 1 will serve to illustrate.

Each member of the senior administration has two roles in the planning process: first, to participate in collegewide planning efforts; second, to guide planning efforts in the units for which he or she is directly accountable. In the evaluation and planning stages, most of the work is done by senior managers and trustees. In the resource allocation and financial planning stages, faculty and administrative department heads participate actively in determining what specific objectives will be set and how they will be achieved.

Figure 1. The Planning Process: A Timetable

Stage	Start	Complete	Chief Financial Officer, Participants
Evaluation	June	August	
Programs			Department Heads
Institution			Senior Managers
Planning	August	December	
Mission			Trustees
Goals			Senior Managers
Strategies			Senior Managers
Resource Allocation	October	December	
Proposed Action Plans			Department Heads
Revised Action Plans			Senior Managers
Financial Planning	December	March	
Multiyear			Department Heads, Chief Financial Officer
Budget Year			Department heads, Chief Financial Officer

Personal Computers in the Planning Process

When computer-based simulation models were first used to support the planning process, all computers were large, expensive, and accessible only to programmers. Later, time-shared systems were developed, and "friendly" interactive software allowed general managers to enter figures from a cathode-ray tube terminal. However, the cost of developing the software was extremely high. Often, more than $50,000 was required to purchase and tailor a program to the needs of the particular college. The process of modifying the computer program, known as software maintenance, was expensive because it required the services of a programmer, who was familiar with the language in which the system was written. However, the advent of the personal computer has made the task of modeling college operations and finances considerably more accessible to senior administrators. This increased access reflects two parallel and related trends: the creation of packaged software and the development of low-cost desk-top hardware.

The development of English-speaking or user-friendly software packages has allowed general managers and other nonprogrammers to create their own models simply by describing the kinds of operating and financial relationships that they wish to model. At least three software packages are well suited to college financial modeling: Multiplan, published by Microsoft, which retails for $275; Lotus 1-2-3, published by Lotus Development Corporation, which retails for $495; and Micro-DSS/Finance, published by Addison-Wesley, which retails for $1,500. Learning times vary from package to package. The typical first-time user is a manager or professional who has no prior experience in using a personal computer. However, a half-day seminar can enable a new user to build a sophisticated financial and operations model of a college within roughly a week, provided that the necessary data have been gathered and analyzed to identify key relationships.

The second trend making possible the development of models to support strategic and financial models is the advent of low-cost desk-top personal computer hardware. Figure 2 displays the types of hardware needed to run the software packages identified in the preceding paragraph. The costs displayed in Figure 2 include not only software and computer hardware but also required peripheral equipment, such as video monitors, disk storage drives, and printers. To these figures must be added an allowance for equipment mantenance and supplies of roughly $1,000 per year. The charge for a half-day training session covering any one of these systems is roughly $250.

The personal computer provides college administrators with an accessible means of supporting the planning process. To what stages of the process can this support be applied? It is applicable in stages two — analyzing major strategic alternatives — three — evaluating the financial feasibility of action plans proposed by faculty and other department heads — and four — developing detailed multiyear financial plans and budget guidelines. Throughout the process, managers' efforts will be aided by the ability to analyze competing proposals for changes in program operations in a short time. In some cases, the personal computer can be used in the room where members of the senior management team consider alternative plans. Two packages, Lotus 1-2-3 and DSS/Finance, not only produce printouts of text and numbers but allow results to be displayed graphically as bar, line, or pie charts.

Figure 2. Hardware Needed to Run Preferred Planning Software

Software Package	Hardware Options	Range of Total System Costs
Multiplan	IBM PC, Apple IIe, Dec VT-100	$3,500–$4,000
Lotus 1-2-3	IBM PC, Compaq Portable	$4,500–$5,500
Micro-DSS/Finance	IBM PC, Apple IIe	$5,000–$6,000

John C. Merson, former Woodrow Wilson Foundation administrative intern at Lenoir-Rhyne College, is vice-president for marketing at The Computer Factory, Inc.

It is the president's job to point out, remind, and persuade;
to suggest new ideas; and to identify places where improvement
is needed and aspects of the operation with which he is not
yet satisfied.

The Presidency of a Small College

Dan C. West

Much of the current literature on college presidents has to do with how a college searches for one. Little seems to have been written about what the presidential candidate should look for in a college. Candidates should give more thought to this issue. So should colleges, since they would attract and retain better presidents if they did. I think that a presidential candidate should be concerned about six areas of the college's character and operation: the board of trustees, the faculty and curriculum, the present student body, resources, staff, and constituent relations. I have listed these areas in the order of their importance.

What is the composition of the board of trustees? How are board members chosen? What is the board leadership like? Is the chairman a strong leader? Does he or she have influence and the board's respect? Does he or she put as much of his or her own time and money into the college as other trustees do? What about the members of the executive committee? Is the committee composed mostly of the stronger trustees? How much do board members give? The prospective president should see the contribution record of each individual trustee. Most boards tell a presidential candidate that they expect him or her to raise money—a lot of money—but how much will the trustees themselves pledge toward the needed amount? Unless they are prepared to put up a substantial amount themselves—between one fourth and one third—why should they expect the president to do so, and why should anyone want to seek money on their behalf? Finally, what do the trustees expect of the new presi-

A. J. Falender and J. C. Merson (Eds.). *Management Techniques for Small and Specialized Institutions.*
New Directions for Higher Education, no. 42. San Francisco: Jossey-Bass, June 1983.

dent? How will they judge him or her? How and when will they determine whether the president has done a satisfactory job?

How strong and how stable are faculty? What percentage is tenured? How many faculty members have a scholarly reputation outside the college? How many are regarded as exceptional teachers within the institution? How well do they function as a group? In particular, how well do they control the quality and effectiveness of the academic program? Further, how good is the curriculum? When was it last evaluated and revised? Does it make sense as a whole, or is it a smorgasbord? What is it expected to produce in graduates? How is it evaluated? How is it improved when improvement is necessary?

Where does the present student body come from? What is the college's main competition for students? What are the demographics of the area from which most students come? What do students do after they graduate? How many persist to graduation? What do they think of the college?

What are the college's resources? A presidential candidate should obtain a copy of the last audit and should go over it carefully, preferably with an accountant who is familiar with college fund accounting and who is not connected with the college. Who are the top five donors to the college? How much have they been giving? Will they make large, challenge type pledges for the current fund campaign? Have they named the college in their wills? Does anyone know how much might be realized in the future from deferred gifts? Has cash flow been a problem? What line of credit does the college have with banks, whether local or elsewhere? How much endowment is there? Has any of it been spent? Why? Who authorized its expenditure? How much is left? How is it invested? Who manages it? Is all the endowment under the college's control, or is some controlled by individuals who remit whatever they decide to the college? What has the endowment been earning? If it has not been earning a respectable average percentage, what is the reason? How much deferred maintenance is there? Will some buildings have to be abandoned, repaired, or declared unsafe? How much will it take to put the college back into top shape? How big is the college's financial aid budget? It should total no more than 12 percent of the total educational and general budget. How much of the financial aid budget is unfunded? That is, how much of the financial aid budget is underwritten by designated endowment income or by federal and state financial aid or gift income? The unfunded amount is really a discount and potentially part of an operating deficit. Finally, how successful has the college been in obtaining gifts from private donors, a sponsoring church body, and foundations? How successful has it been in obtaining grants from the federal government?

The next consideration is the staff. What are the capacities and abilities of executive-level staff—deans, business manager, and vice-presidents? How well are they performing at present? Will it be possible to replace them if that seems necessary? Who is the president's secretary? Is she or he good? Does she or he maintain confidentiality? Can she or he be replaced if necessary? What are admissions staff like? What is their track record? How long have they been at the college? What are development staff like? How much have they been raising? Where does the money come from—church, foundations, individuals, alumni, corporations?

Finally, what kind of relationship does the college have with its constituents—local community, donors, alumni, sponsoring church body, business community, and home state? Is there support for the college within the local community? Are there any big donors in the local community? What is the attitude of community leaders and local school officials? What is the attitude of local vendors? Are there any long-time contributors who have given consistently for many years? What percentage of the alumni contributes? What is the nature of the relationship between the college and the sponsoring church? What is the attitude of prominent church leaders? Are there any strong congregations who are warm toward the college? What about the local congregation?

Some of these questions may seem extremely blunt. Unless they are answered, however, the successful candidate may not be able to be a successful president. Moreover, unless the search committee is willing and able to supply satisfactory answers, its members may not understand their situation well enough to identify the person best qualified to meet its needs. Candidates should not worry about appearing too hard-nosed or demanding. If you are wanted, you are in the strongest position during the interview process that you will ever be in with the college. If you are not wanted, the quality of the answers that you receive to these questions will make that clear. If trustees are put off by such questions, they do not understand the challenge of leading a small college today.

There is a serious need today to strengthen the procedures by which academic administrators are selected (Blyn and Zoerner, 1982). This is especially true for the presidents of small colleges. One of the places where improvement is most needed lies in the questions asked of the college. It is probably wise for the candidate for the presidency of a small college to insist on meeting with both faculty and the entire board of trustees, so that he or she has an opportunity to interview both groups as well as to be interviewed by them.

When the small college has made its choice and a candidate has been selected, what next? What are the chief responsibilities of the president of a small college? One of the president's main responsibilities is to understand that he or she cannot do everything. You have to make some important choices about the most effective use of your limited time and finite energy. For the small-college president, I rank fund raising first. I do not particularly like that. I would prefer to put educational leadership or spending time with students or long-range planning ahead of fund raising, but the truth of the matter is that, however well a small-college president does all those things, his tenure will probably be short if he cannot raise money.

Historically, small colleges have depended on income from tuition and raised from private sources. Particularly since World War II, independent colleges have had to mount constant campaigns to obtain money, both for operating expenses and for capital development (Mayhew, 1962). As a result, the inability or the unwillingness to raise money has been the single most important factor in the downfall of unsuccessful small-college presidents. If a president can raise money, he or she will have an excellent chance of winning the respect and support both of the board and of the faculty. A president cannot survive without such respect and support. Thus, I think of fund raising as establishing one's base. The way to do it is to hire a first-rate development officer, make sure that he or she is willing to call on people and ask them for money, see that someone on the development staff is doing development research, and then set out to choose and cultivate the individuals for whom you as president will be personally responsible.

Seventy-five percent of all private gifts to higher education are contributed by 5 percent of the donors (Smith, 1975). Every president should determine early in his or her administration the hundred individuals whose support can make the difference for the future of the college (Frantzreb, 1975). Presidential fund-raising time must be spent where it counts most. The development officer should study the market and identify the top 1 percent of the prospective givers. They should become the object of the president's attention (Francis, 1975).

In recent years, income from the federal government, mostly in the form of student financial aid, has become a large part of the funds needed to finance the small colleges. This means that small-college presidents have to be good managers of their admissions and financial aid offices. If enrollment is a critical problem, then the director of admissions and the director of financial aid should both report directly to the president. The alternative is to have a vice-president for marketing who understands the role of each administrator and who can coordinate their efforts with fund raising, public relations, and the other aspects of marketing. Most small colleges do not yet have such a person on their staff, so the president must accept personal responsibility for oversight of these functions. After all, the income from tuition and fees, including the large amount that accrues to the college in the form of state and federal aid, is usually larger than the sum being raised by the development office.

Just as the failure to raise money from private sources has been the biggest trap for presidents in the past, the worst pitfall today is the unwillingness or the inability to understand and manage the marketing of the college — not only fund raising but also public relations, image building, constituency participation, design and packaging of curriculum and extracurriculum, recruitment, financial aid, and retention. I reiterate, however, that the central element is the ability to ask people for money and success in getting it.

The next most important responsibility of the president lies in his or her relationship with the board of trustees. That relationship is the presidential power base. In the governance of any educational institution, the functions of the board and president are intimately and inseparably related. The board's behavior profoundly affects the president's performance (Nason and Axelrod, 1980). Without the confidence and strong backing of the board, a president is vulnerable; the president has no natural allies in the faculty, which is the other powerful group in a college. With strong backing from trustees, a president can weather many a storm. Faculty know whether a president has the respect of the board, and students take their cues from faculty.

Strong board support is a function of success in fund raising efforts; stable enrollments; good management of resources, which includes balanced budgets; and effectiveness in building the college image. To this must be added the establishment and nurturance of personal relationships with at least a majority of the trustees, and these relationships must be marked by mutual respect and admiration. Presidents have to keep in direct contact with trustees. Letters, telephone calls, visits, and committee work are all in order. Three or four times a year, I send a newsletter to all trustees and other special friends and major donors of the college. The newsletter is written in an informal style, and I make it clear to the reader that it was composed by me. The trustees are my bosses as well as my patrons, and I have to keep them informed. Presidents have been known to suffer a surprise no-confidence vote at a board meeting because they had not kept in touch with their trustees.

I regard the board as the core group of the college's fund-raising base. On behalf of the nominations committee of our board, I personally interview all prospective trustees, informing them of our expectations — regular attendance at meetings, advocacy of the college, help in recruiting and fund raising, and an annual personal contribution — should they accept nomination and election. Thus, trustees begin their service knowing what they will be asked to do.

About half of the prospective trustees decline, feeling that they cannot or do not want to give as much time, effort, or money as we expect. When this happens, I consider that both the college and prospective trustee are ahead.

Every year, after making my own pledge, I personally solicit each trustee for his or her gift to the annual fund, the capital fund, or both, and I thank all the trustees for their gifts with individual handwritten letters. For several years running, our board has contributed approximately one third of the money for each annual current fund drive and for the last three capital campaigns.

We work for 100 percent participation each year by the entire board. This accomplishes three things. First, it strengthens the hand of the president and others who ask other prospective givers for donations, since it shows how much those who own the college really care about it. Second, it has the effect of keeping bench warmers off the board and of deepening the commitment and involvement of trustees, since we all tend to care more about the organizations into which we put our own money. Third, it tends to pull trustees and president together into a deeper relationship of mutual caring about the institution, since all are investing their own time, talent, and money in the same cause and thus in each other. The sense of satisfaction and accomplishment that is gained by president and trustees alike solidifies their relationship. Thus, the fund-raising responsibility and the trustee relationship responsibility are symbiotic and close to the heart of what makes a successful small-college presidency.

With proven success in fund raising and solid support from the board, the small-college president is in a strong position to exert creative leadership on campus and to influence the fashioning of the educational program. Some people would argue that this responsibility, which I have placed third, is the most important. That may be true, but the small-college president typically has to earn the right to exercise such responsibility. One must pay one's dues by raising money and by building strong board backing before one can expect to be taken seriously by the campus community and its leaders, the faculty.

How does a president best exercise educational leadership? The president is the one who is most responsible for building and articulating a vision for the college. As Cowley (1980, p. 67) states, "The president. . . is the only person who has a total view of its work. Professors see primarily their own specialties and have glimpses of those of their friends; department heads concentrate upon their departments. . . the trustees primarily give their attention to financial and material matters. No one but the president sees the whole, and hence he or she has the best opportunity and the most insistent obligation to plan for the future. To be equal to this opportunity and to this obligation, the president must be a student of social and educational trends and apply his or her scholarship to the development of the institution at large. The day has passed when college presidents can continue to be scholars in the academic disciplines of their teaching years. Today, they must be students of higher education and of American society."

The president also needs to provide the college with at least a broad outline of the priorities on which public awareness and financial resources are to be focused. This outline includes an articulation of the mission of the college, a determination of the relative emphasis to be given to each goal, and considered judgments about which sources of funding should be approached for current operations, endowment, and buildings (Smith, 1975). Naturally, to accomplish these tasks, I must enlist the participation and seek the consensus of all the important constituencies of the college — trustees, faculty, students, staff, and alumni — but it is clearly my responsibility to see that the mission, the goals, and the strategies are formulated, adopted, and implemented. No one else is in a better position to do this.

It is hard to be a visionary and a planner. Colleges are faced with a myriad of forces totally beyond their control. Still, there must be a vision of what is to be (Wenrich, 1980). Faculty respond best to a clearly articulated vision of the college's future that a strong president has put together. Faculty function least successfully in the face of insecurity and uncertainty. By definition, their work requires them to concentrate on a limited set of concerns and to focus their reading on a narrow area. Unless they feel that the presiding officer is secure in his or her job and has a clear idea of where the institution is headed, they will react in ways that are hurtful both to themselves and to the college.

However, it has been my experience of ten years as a small-college president that faculty work best if I give direction in a broad way, pointing out places where improvement is needed, calling for a new program, suggesting a study to determine how best to reallocate resources. Thus, when I have suggested that the core curriculum needs revision or that we need an honors program to challenge our best students or when I have wondered aloud whether all our concentrations can still be justified, faculty have responded with sound and creative new approaches that work. In contrast, when I have gotten involved in detail, as in the actual construction of a new program, the results have often been unsatisfactory. I can point to the wreckage of a failed calendar revision and to an unsuccessful annual faculty workshop plan, among others, as evidence of that.

Not surprisingly, faculty usually insist on being the architects of programs and policies that they themselves will have to carry out. But, they will respond to broad objectives that are clearly articulated and clearly consistent with the overall direction and mission of the institution. I have to resist the temptation to get involved in the fine points of an academic program. I have an opportunity to fine-tune as the design proceeds; everyone is clear about the president's authority to veto or simply not to recommend to the board. But, the actual construction is best left to the faculty, since they will not do anything that they do not like to do anyway.

I think that this last point is both very important for a successful presidency and close to the heart of understanding the difference between mere management and leadership in higher education. Management is the art of allocating resources within an organization in a manner designed to reach its goals (Cyert, 1980). This is a terribly important responsibility, and it carries a lot of power, but it is also possible to take all one's cues in allocating resources from what others have already said or done. Leadership can be distinguished from management as the art of stimulating human resources within an organization to concentrate on total organizational goals rather than on individual or subgroup goals (Cyert, 1980).

The difficulty of educational leadership in a small college should not be taken for granted. The academy is surely the most difficult of organizations to manage well. Institutional objectives have to be much more vaguely defined in the academic environment than they are in business or even in government. High productivity is nearly impossible. Anything done quickly — even the most insignificant task — becomes suspect (Blyn and Zoerner, 1982). The successful education leader-president will search for and find an agreement between himself or herself and faculty in the governance of the college. For example, the president and supporting administrative staff may have the authority to fashion institutional objectives, such as defining the market, that the college will serve and designing a strategy for serving that market effectively. The process that this entails might include identifying the clientele to be recruited; the appropriate mix of programs; critical aspects of the delivery system, such as pricing and financial aid; and admissions criteria. For their part, faculty must have the authority to ensure the integrity of the educational process. As a result, they will have responsibility for designing the educational programs, for teaching and administering these programs, for evaluating student performance, and ultimately for attaining the educational objectives (Blyn and Zoerner, 1982). The line between pointing the way or painting the broad strokes on the one hand and trying to impose programs on unwilling faculty on the other is a fine one. It is the difference between leading and meddling.

It helps me to remember that I live somewhere between the present reality and the institution that I expect my college to become in the future. It is therefore my job constantly to point out, remind, and persuade; to suggest new ideas; and to identify places where improvement is needed and aspects of our operation with which we are not yet satisfied. Of course, leadership is as much a question of timing as it is of anything else. It is also true that people can only be led where they want to go. Still, a good leader must have a certain irrational quality, a stubborn refusal to face facts, infectious optimism (Korda, 1981), the ability to convince others that they can do more than they think they can. William Blake wrote in "The Marriage of Heaven and Hell," that "What is now proved was once only imagin'd." Someone has to imagine for a small college, and the president is in the best position to do it.

College presidents have been in danger of becoming mere consensus takers (Ness, 1971). Of course, participatory democracy must remain the ideal on every campus, both in theory and in practice. Participative decision making, however, needs a carefully worked out agenda, it needs to be sharply focused on analyzing a clearly defined problem, and it must be carried out with a commitment to results that are solutions (Maccoby, 1980).

The professorial establishment is so designed as generally to militate against substantial change in the status quo (Ness, 1971). Yet, as Cardinal Newman has been quoted as saying (Greenleaf, 1980), "To live is to change; to live well is to have changed often." Small colleges simply have to change. They have to adapt, improve, revise, and build if they are to do more than just survive. I think that small colleges can change if a strong president and a dedicated faculty can work out the right mix of presidential and faculty responsibility. The best way of accomplishing this aim is to agree at the outset that neither is more important than the other: Each has a different responsibility and different authority with which to carry it out. As Cleveland (1971, pp. 23–24) observes, "The hallmarks of effective [leadership] are the soft voice and the low key, the search for consensus [rather than choosing up sides and voting], the constructive use of ambiguity, a can-do spirit unwarranted by expert predictions, a willingness to take the initiative and see others get the credit. . . the most effective leadership doesn't show, and [it] especially. . . doesn't show off."

If a small-college president can raise money, secure board backing, and provide effective educational leadership, he or she is well along the way to successful tenure. The small-college president has major responsibility: the need to find, hire, motivate, and coordinate talented administrators. Many presidents, vice-presidents, and deans seem to assume that administrators can be ignored until something goes wrong—a strategy that guarantees that something will go wrong (Hodgkinson, 1981). An institution or organization that loses its capacity to attract the kinds of people whom it needs is on its way down. If this happens, a president ends up putting the wrong people into top management positions. The wrong people are people who can only keep the machinery running. The right people are people who can help to achieve the organization's purposes. With the wrong people in place, the center of administration can shift from the main functions to the support functions. This is one of the most dangerous things that can happen to an institution (Drucker, 1967).

Choosing and directing the executive-level administrators is one of the most important things that I do. I must depend on these persons to implement policy made by the board and by faculty, to organize and direct the programs and departments of the college, to motivate the people who direct or teach or provide support, and to solve the problems that inevitably occur. There should be a high degree of trust, communication, and mutual respect between me and each executive who reports directly to me. I try to find ways to build rapport with these people, to reward, support, and praise them. They get little thanks from faculty or students. Their work is largely invisible to trustees and other constituents. Yet their work is critically important; they can make or break the president. It seems unfair that a college president can get the credit for the results of the work of an able dean, admissions director, or development executive, but it is just as unfair that presidents often get blamed for the shortcomings of these people.

The importance of the work of comptrollers, directors of admission, and vice-presidents for development is fairly obvious. Less obvious, and therefore more worthy of mention, is the need for an able dean of students who can direct the extracurriculum and the auxiliary enterprises with talent and businesslike skill and for a vice-president or director of evaluation and planning who can gather and assemble data in a manner that facilitates problem solving, innovation, and long-range planning. How can a president and his or her executives provide vision and leadership without such information?

Of course, the dean of the college is foremost in importance. He or she has to be handpicked by the president, even if he or she is chosen from a list drawn up by a search committee. The dean occupies both a line and a staff position (Mayhew, 1962). That is, as adviser on academic and staff matters, as liaison between the president and faculty, and as staff person for the education committee of the board, the dean is staff. As second in charge and as the person responsible for the campus in the absence of the president, as supervisor and leader of the faculty, and as a member of the executive staff of the college with responsibility for carrying out policies, the dean also has line authority. Thus, a good dean is essential. A good dean understands faculty but is willing to transcend their collective interests. A good dean must be instantly alert to defend faculty but just as ready to defend the president. Most of all, a dean must know how to touch base, mend fences, play the game, and still get the work done. He or she must understand the covert nature of faculty politics well enough to effect change anyway. In my opinion, it is hard to take too much trouble to find the right dean, hard to overestimate the importance of having a good dean, and hard to praise an effective dean enough.

How do you tell when an executive staff person is doing a good job? Goals should be formulated for each major program and service that an executive heads. Objectives should then be set to indicate how much of the goal is to be realized within a specific time period. Thus, the three key words are *assign, measure,* and *reward.* Performance should be measured against plans. Measurement and evaluation of performance should become the test of executive effectiveness. A fully computerized management intelligence system should show plans made and results achieved to date in such areas as student recruitment and admissions, academic programs, fund raising, and financial operations (Merson and Qualls, 1979).

In the preceding pages, I have suggested that fund raising, trustee relations, educational leadership, and effectiveness in hiring executives are the most important responsibilities of the small-college president. Unfortunately, small colleges are more dependent on presidential leadership than large ones are. Small colleges are usually understaffed. If someone does not look at things with a broad scope and worry about the future, the small college will stagnate, then slip behind. Small colleges are thus more vulnerable than large institutions to ineffective leadership from the president's office. Search committees should focus more on track record, proven ability to obtain results, and needed personal qualities than on credentials, the stature of recommenders, and academic reputation.

The scrutiny of my performance by our board did not stop when I was hired as the new president. I developed a written job description and asked that I be evaluated annually. If this has not been the practice at the institution, the new college president should insist on it and help to institute it. In any case, it is never too late. It is important because it allows you to know where you stand and how you can do a better job. Moreover, the president who takes the initiative in establishing a format for evaluation of his or her performance will be in a position to introduce a discussion of the conditions under which a graceful exit from the presidency can occur—when the board or the president decides that this is desirable (Fisk and Richardson, 1980). A plan for the president's exit should receive as much advance thought as a contingency plan for the college in the event of enrollment or economic declines.

In my own case, the executive committee of the board has the responsibility for evaluating my performance annually. A form is sent to each trustee on the committee, who checks off ratings and fills in blanks with narrative comments. The chairman of the board, who is also chair of the executive committee, receives these forms, collates the results, and prepares a summary for me that averages the ratings in each category and that reports all the comments (their authors are not named). The chairman then meets with me privately to discuss the summary plus other comments that come up in the discussion. The committee meets without me to discuss its evaluation and to set the terms of my compensation for the following year.

These sessions and the summary of board evaluations have taught me a lot. I have discovered, for example, that I am sometimes evaluated on the basis of the performance of those who report to me. I have learned about weaknesses and faults of which I was not even aware. I have learned a lot about management, since most members of the executive committee are business executives or professionals and experienced in executive-level management. Many comments are extremely apt, but the authors have been reluctant to make them to me directly because of tact.

The other important measure of my own performance is the president's annual written report. Now the size of a book, this report covers all aspects of the college's operation for the previous fiscal year. It is required by our board's bylaws. I have chosen to ask each executive to draft a chapter on his or her administrative component. I write the chapter on my own activities. After reading and editing all the drafts, I write an introduction that summarizes and evaluates the condition of the college and the progress made during the previous year. I try to be as candid about the problems and failures as I am about the successes. The report gives trustees a detailed look at my own performance and the results. Preparing it requires me to record and reflect on what has occurred, and this process provides the basis for developing our objectives for the following year. Finally, the report is an invaluable historical record, both of my own work and of college development.

The rewards of a small-college presidency can be very great. As a result of its size and scale, the small college can be more amenable to leadership than the large college, and one can see positive development and progress from year to year that can be source of great satisfaction. Moreover, it is possible within a few years to be responsible for most selections of persons in key administrative positions. It is possible to play a key role in shaping the composition of the board of trustees. It is possible to build a long-range plan that can guide the course of the college for years to come. It is possible to mold the composition of the student body, to influence the shape of the curriculum, to have a key role in selecting many faculty, and even to change the face of the campus. Such changes are possible depending on the effectiveness with which the small-college president carries out the four key responsibilities indicated here. The president who is able to make such changes for the better feels great pride and joy. However, the risks are also great. Neglect of family and health;

adversity created by factors beyond one's control; political mistakes that create a campus crisis so severe that resignation is the only recourse; arrogance caused by feelings of indispensability, infallibility, or invulnerability; or just staying on too long are some of the greatest risks.

I subscribe to the proposition that no one should remain longer than ten years. Of course, everything depends on the particular college and on the individual who is president, but in almost every case one will be fresh out of new ideas after that period of time. As the end of my ninth year approached, I was offered another presidency. I knew it was time to leave, but I was not really attracted to the other institution. I wanted to stay, but I knew it was unfair both to the college and to me if I did. The solution was a year-long sabbatical. Only in that way, I felt, could I come back refreshed and invigorated with new insights and energy and thus in good conscience stay a few years more. Fortunately, our board agreed. One of our ablest trustees agreed to be acting president, and I literally left for a whole year. It worked beautifully and taught both the college and me that not even the president was indispensable.

Sabbaticals, leaves, mandatory vacations, study leaves, and professional development opportunities should be insisted on by the board of trustees. When well planned, they are cheaper than the search for a new president, which at best is a risky undertaking. Some small colleges may not be able to afford the luxury of changing chief executive officers every few years (Hesburgh, 1979). Timing is important, as with anything else, but presidents who wait for just the right time to take a sabbatical will never take one. I suggest that, after six or seven years, a president and a board should begin looking for a way to begin a sabbatical or else look toward making a graceful exit.

The presidency of a small college is no place for maintainers, shy people, or prestige seekers. Small colleges are next to the bottom in the prestige pecking order of higher education, and the work load of thankless tasks more than earns whatever perks and glory are attached to the job. However, for the man or woman who does not mind asking others to help support a college, who enjoys people, who likes change, who is able to make decisions, and who thrives on challenge, the small college can be one of the most interesting and enjoyable organizations to lead that I can imagine. It is one of the last remaining places in our society where an individual can make a profound difference.

References

Blyn, M. R., and Zoerner, C. E., Jr. "The Academic Strong Pushers: The Origins of the Upcoming Crisis in the Management of Academia." *Change,* 1982, *14,* 21–25, 60.

Cleveland, H. "The Education of Administrators for Higher Education." Fourth David D. Henry Lecture at the University of Illinois at Urbana–Champaign, April 1977.

Cowley, W. H. *Presidents, Professors, and Trustees: The Evolution of American Academic Government.* San Francisco: Jossey-Bass, 1980.

Cyert, R. M. "Managing Universities in the 1980s." In C. Argyris and R. M. Cyert (Eds.), *Leadership in the 80s.* Cambridge, Mass.: Institute for Educational Management, Harvard University, 1980.

Drucker, P. F., "What Principles of Management Can the President of a Small College Use to Improve the Efficiency of His Institution?" In E. J. McGrath (Ed.), *Selected Issues in College Administration.* New York: Teachers College Press, 1967.

Fisk, E. C., and Richardson, R. C., Jr. "Presidential Evaluation: The State of the Art." *Liberal Education,* Fall 1979, Association of American Colleges as quoted in *Presidential Leadership for the 1980s,* resource notebook for the 25th National Institute, Council for the Advancement of Small Colleges, June 1980.

Francis, N. C. "The President's Management Role in Development." In *The President's Role in Development.* Washington, D.C.: Association of American Colleges, 1975.

Frantzreb, A. C. "Elements of a Development Program." In *The President's Role in Development.* Washington, D.C.: Association of American Colleges, 1975.

Greenleaf, R. K. "Excerpts from Servant: Retrospect and Prospect." In *Presidential Leadership for the 1980s,* resource notebook for the 25th National Institute, Council for the Advancement of Small Colleges, June, 1980.

Hesburgh, T. "The College Presidency: Life Between a Rock and a Hard Place." *Change,* 1979, *11* (4), 43-47.

Hodgkinson, H. L. "Administrative Development." In A. W. Chickering and Associates, *The Modern American College: Responding to the New Realities of Diverse Students and a Changing Society.* San Francisco· Jossey-Bass, 1981.

Korda, M. "How to Be a Leader." *Newsweek,* January 5, 1981, p. 7.

Maccoby, M. "Leadership Needs of the 1980s." In *Current Issues in Higher Education.* Washington, D.C.: American Association for Higher Education, 1979. As quoted in *Presidential Leadership for the 1980s,* resource notebook for the 25th National Institute, Council for the Advancement of Small Colleges, June 1980.

Mayhew, L. B. *The Smaller Liberal Arts College.* Washington, D.C.: Center for Applied Research in Education, 1962.

Merson, J. C., and Qualls, R. L. *Strategic Planning for Colleges and Universities: A Systems Approach to Planning and Resource Allocation.* San Antonio: Trinity University Press, 1979.

Nason, J. W., and Axelrod, N. R. *Presidential Assessment: A Challenge to College and University Leadership.* Washington, D.C.: Association of Governing Boards of Universities and Colleges, 1980.

Ness, F. W. *An Uncertain Glory.* San Francisco: Jossey-Bass, 1971.

Smith, G. T. "Developing Private Support: Three Issues." In *The President's Role in Development.* Washington, D.C.: Association of American Colleges, 1975.

Wenrich, J. W. "All Things to All People?" *Community and Junior College Journal,* 1980, *51,* 37-40.

Dan C. West has been president of Arkansas College since 1972.

Develop the case statement first. Then, put leaders in place who can direct the capital campaign. Finally, match fund-raising techniques with the prospect market.

Some Notes on Fund Raising

Robert J. Corcoran

Planning a successful fund-raising campaign for capital gifts presupposes the proper mixture of three essential elements: a clear and convincing case for support; the requisite leadership for planning, mounting, and conducting the campaign; and the cultivation, which is to say the persuasion, of appropriate donors who can make the type of gifts needed. Each element is as important as each of the legs of a camera tripod; if one of the legs is weak, the effort, like the camera that the tripod supports, will wobble.

A development committee comprised of key members of the governing board and institutional management should have the responsibility for overseeing the fund-raising program. An important first step for the committee is preparation of the case statement.

The Case Statement

No broad-based solicitation of gifts should be undertaken until the reasons for the appeal and the reasonableness of the appeal have been understood, agreed upon, and enunciated. The case statement is the basic document, the official source of information for those involved in the project and for those who will be asked to contribute to the project. It need not be an elaborate publication, but it should answer all the important questions, describe the need clearly, review the arguments for support, and explain the proposed plan. The case statement should also outline how gifts are to be made, what gift ranges

A. J. Falender and J. C. Merson (Eds.). *Management Techniques for Small and Specialized Institutions.*
New Directions for Higher Education, no. 42. San Francisco: Jossey-Bass, June 1983.

are needed, and who will vouch for the project and give it leadership and direction. The case statement should raise sights, provide perspective, promote a sense of history and continuity, and convey the importance, relevance, and urgency of the project.

Most people will not contribute to causes that they do not clearly understand. What is needed? Why is it needed? Why is it needed now? How much will it cost? Why is the institution worthy of support? Where is it going from here? Unless and until there are clear and convincing answers to all these questions and others like them, efforts to obtain anything but token support will probably fail.

Since the case statement reflects and projects institutional philosophy, policies, and objectives, it is obvious that the governing board can best determine what goes into it. Another important reason for involving the board is that the self-study process required to develop the case statement can lead to the discovery of institutional weaknesses hitherto unnoticed or ignored. These weaknesses must receive attention before a campaign for outside support can be undertaken. The reader can be quite sure that those who are to be asked for major gifts will look very carefully at what and how the institution is doing internally before they will give.

For example, the quality of the institution's educational programs is of great interest to alumni, corporations, and foundations, three sources that in 1981 (the latest year for which statistics are available) supplied 65 percent — $2749 billion — of the financial support that American colleges and universities received. The reasons are not far to seek. Alumni have a natural interest in preserving the worth and prestige of their own degrees. Corporations and foundations want to be sure that they will not be throwing good money after bad. Is the college known for its academic excellence? Can any of its programs be called truly distinctive? Have graduates made a mark in their community?

Some people require reassurance about the operating efficiency of nonprofit organizations. Can it be demonstrated that the institution is well-managed? Are strict budgetary controls maintained, or is it sometimes necessary to dip into endowment principal in order to meet operating costs? Foundations and corporations tend to look askance at the practice unless there are extraordinary extenuating circumstances. Is the college making reasonable efforts to utilize its plant more efficiently through extracurricular use? Many schools and colleges are discovering that they can realize added earned income from on-campus academic and business conferences, from year-round programs of continuing education for the community, and from the practice of making residential accommodations available to outsiders during vacation periods. Academic prestige is important, of course, but it is the rare donor of a large gift who will not be warmed by what he sees as careful business management and efficient use of facilities.

Discovering how others perceive the institution can be a valuable part of the self-evaluation required to prepare the case statement. Questionnaires mailed to alumni and parents (anonymous responses are to be preferred) can be very revealing. So, too, can person-to-person opinion polls in the local community. This latter effort can have double effect: Reactions and suggestions can be helpful in themselves, and those who are polled will be gratified because they have been asked. That can be very positive public relations. A good many institutions, it should be noted, make it a practice before launching a major campaign to retain fund-raising counsel to conduct an in-depth feasibility study among a select group—usually a minimum of fifty persons—that includes alumni, friends, local community and business leaders, and foundation officials, among others. In this way, the market can be tested, reactions to the institution and its programs and plans can be elicited, and strengths and weaknesses can be discovered at a relatively modest cost.

Having satisfied yourself that the house is in order, you can begin to set down the written case statement. Ideally, the case statement should be the joint work of the president and development staff—the former because he or she knows what needs to be said, the latter because they usually have the writing skill to say it clearly, concretely, and persuasively. All too many case statements are platitudinous and dull when they should and could be informative and inspiring. Of course, you should emphasize institutional strengths and accomplishments, but you should also avoid exaggerated claims and unrealistic plans. Face up to institutional weaknesses, and explain what you are doing to correct them. Present an unvarnished picture of your financial resources and your annual operating costs. Explain your plan or program in full detail. If your project involves physical facilities, try to include before and after illustrations. Above all, avoid producing what reads like a college catalogue; the objective is to stimulate interest, not to put the reader to sleep.

Institutional Leadership

The second necessary ingredient is strong and exemplary leadership. The leadership and effectiveness of any fund-raising campaign begins with the board and the chairman chosen to direct the campaign. These persons are expected to set the pace for other donors and to recruit additional leadership for soliciting gifts. They lead because they are convinced of the merits of the cause, and they support it personally for the same reason. Their cultivation of donors, their screening of prospects, and their willingness to give and to seek gifts will be the key to the program's success.

The importance of strong leadership for the campaign cannot be overemphasized. Because the right general chairman can be the biggest single factor in the success of a campaign for capital gifts, he or she must be selected with great care. The general chairman may be (and most often is) a member of the institution's board. It is helpful when the general chairman is a member of the family who understands the inner workings of the institution and who has been involved long enough to have a thorough grasp of the institution's strengths and weaknesses. Moreover, the general chairman should be known and respected by your constituency, capable of making a meaningful gift, able to devote sufficient time to the campaign, able to enlist key people in leadership roles in the campaign, prepared to participate personally in solicitation of pace-setting gifts when appropriate, able to be a public spokesman for the institution, and able to motivate a campaign organization. The ideal general chairman is one who offers by words, deeds, and financial support an example that inspires high standards of performance among all those who work on the campaign. This is a tall order, but the result almost always is a broad response of enthusiastic support.

The Prospect Market

The typical fund-raising campaign operates on one or the other of two time-honored principles: Either 80 to 85 percent of the goal will come from 10 to 15 percent of the donors, or the top ten gifts should meet one third of the goal, the next hundred gifts should meet the second third of the goal, while the balance of the prospects should meet the bottom third of the goal. Either way, it is clear that devoting a good deal of time to the care, feeding, and eventual solicitation of major donors makes a good deal of sense.

However, before the major donors can be solicited, they must be identified. Presumably, your annual giving program has given you some clues about individual feelings and attitudes toward the institution. Those who have demonstrated their interest and concern by sending dollars for annual operation or library purchases are obvious candidates for larger capital gifts directed at a major institutional purpose. You will have the job of raising their sights considerably, but at least you know they are in your corner. If you have been doing your homework and keeping track of alumni accomplishments and activities, you will have a fair idea about those who are able but not yet ready or willing. Finally, there are those whom you are not sure about. They may have it, and they may not.

For all these individuals, you need in-depth screening and rating. Enlist groups of knowledgeable alumni—by class, geographical location, or both—and ask them to go over the names with a fine-tooth comb. Classmates and business and professional associates can often provide a mine of information about the financial circumstances of fellow alumni. Ask those who do the screening and rating to express an opinion on the possible response of each person on your list and to suggest his or her giving potential in dollars. Be prepared to add some names and to drop others. There may be some surprises and disappointments.

It can be a good idea to seek the help of administrative staff and faculty in the screening and rating process. They may well have insights into the special interests of certain prospects. Once given the appropriate leads, development office staff will often be able to uncover additional information about individual alumni prospects through a number of standard business, professional, and financial directories and other public sources.

Cultivation and involvement together make up the next step. The formation of a leadership society or gift club can be useful. Becoming a member of a President's Club (the name can vary) by contributing $1,000 or more can appeal to many donors, especially if membership carries with it such perquisites as an invitation to the president's annual dinner or reception. Everyone appreciates public recognition. And, of course, everyone who joins has had his or her sights raised. Very important, too, are the alumni-oriented events during the year. The annual alumni reunion, particularly the twenty-fifth and the fiftieth reunions, do much to renew old friendships and to rekindle old enthusiasms for alma mater. I have often thought that the typical five-year span between reunions is too long. It may be true that everyone will not come every year, but there is no harm in asking. Moreover, if they can anticipate a program that is intellectually and academically interesting as well as social, a good many will come more often.

The cultivation of parents should not be overlooked. It may well be argued that the parent of moderate means is already hard pressed to meet what he or she may view as exorbitant tuition—at least in comparison with what it cost when the parent was a student—but not all parents are struggling to pay tuition, and those who are thought able to make a gift should certainly be cultivated. The way is made much smoother, of course, if particular attention is paid to the parents of students who are doing well academically.

If you do not have alumni clubs in various areas where alumni live and work, takes steps to establish them. If they already exist, keep them strong and cohesive through regular visits by the president and key faculty members. Keep alumni club members up to date on school happenings and policies. Encourage informal dinners and receptions so that alumni have a chance to talk with senior school officials. The best form of cultivation is personal cultivation. Cultivation is an art that includes informing, entertaining, giving recognition, and generally paying attention to those who may be persuaded to offer financial support. Cultivation can mean awards, personal visits, dinners, receptions, seats for athletic events and scholarly lectures, even greeting cards on birthdays and anniversaries. How it is to be accomplished is up to the school. That is must be accomplished cannot be doubted. The person who is thoroughly informed about the school and who is made to understand that he or she is needed and appreciated is the person most likely to reciprocate with a gift.

The approach to corporate prospects is somewhat different. Such prospects are not apt to be caught up in the nostalgia. Their giving is motivated by what they see as the public good and by their own enlightened self-interest. It does no harm, of course, if you have alumni who are members of corporate giving committees or if corporate officials serve on your own board. But, in the main, corporate prospects need to be shown cold facts and figures. If they are made to recognize your academic excellence and the quality of your graduates, they can be persuaded to give. Those who number your graduates among their ranks can be expected to be especially receptive. Your objective should be to keep corporate prospects regularly in touch with what you are doing and how well you are doing it.

Foundations, although they still contribute substantial monies to educational institutions, are not the important factor that they once were. In recent years, many foundations have been giving increasing attention to social services and reducing the size of the pie available to education. This has made the individual slices much smaller. Of course, you should try. But, you should research a foundation carefully so that your request does not fall on deaf ears. Consult foundation annual reports to discover foundation purposes and objectives and to find out where grants went last year. Bear in mind that the competition for foundation grants is keen. But, bear in mind also that there is an important difference between foundations and other giving sources. Alumni, parents, friends, and corporations can choose to give or refuse to give. However, foundations are required to give money away, or they risk dissolution under the law.

Finally, allow me to offer a few discreet suggestions based upon twenty years of fund-raising experience involving scores of nonprofit institutions of all kinds. First, do not launch a large-scale campaign for capital gifts until and unless you have tested the waters—through a successful annual giving program, for example. Second, do your homework thoroughly before embarking on a campaign. A feasibility study can be very valuable in this regard. Third, set your goal at a level that is reasonably attainable. If you exceed it, so much the better, but failure to meet a goal can spell psychological disaster: The next time that you campaign, you will be remembered as a loser. Fourth, remember that appeals to foundations do not require a large and organized volunteer force. Foundation officials seek a sensibly conceived proposal, an appropriate budget, and a clear expression of the need for the project, its goals, and the expected outcomes. Fifth, establish a five-year plan, a two-year plan, and a one-year plan for your institution. These plans do not need to be followed rigidly, but they can serve as sensible guidelines for your development. Sixth, if the development program that you contemplate cannot be met wholly at this time because adequate financial support is not there, consider breaking the program up into several elements and seeking capital gifts in several phases over a period of years. If each element can be shown to be part of an integrated whole, the phased approach can work. Finally, a low-key program soliciting bequests from alumni and friends can be conducted without a formal campaign. So, too, can a program of planned giving—charitable gift annuities, annuity trusts, unitrusts, and pooled income funds. Lawyers among your alumni body can be very helpful here.

Fund raising is hard work. It can also be highly rewarding, both in dollars for the institution and in satisfaction for those who participate as donors and volunteers. As the president of Harvard University said many years ago, good luck and press on.

Robert J. Corcoran is president of Robert J. Corcoran Company, a Boston-based fund-raising consulting firm.

The keys to effective student recruitment are creativity in seeking applicants and mobilization of institutional support for the admissions program.

Student Recruitment and Admissions

Carl Allen

During the next ten years, the president of a small or specialized institution must learn to run an exceptional admissions operation, or he or she will be managing an institution in decline. The college that develops the most creative and effective admissions program will at best maintain the quality of its current student body. To survive the 1980s unscathed, the small college must have a talented admissions director and a president who can marshall the resources of the entire college behind the admissions program.

A Real Shortage

The Western Interstate Commission on Higher Education (WICHE) report (McConnell, 1979), the generally accepted demographic survey, shows that there will be 25 percent fewer students in college in 1992 than there were in 1979. Some regions will experience greater declines than others. For example, the Northeast will experience a 40 percent drop, while a few states in the Southwest will see slight increases. In general, a college should plan on facing a shortage of at least the national average, since colleges in the regions with the greatest declines are making plans to recruit in the more stable areas.

The certainty of declining enrollments and their impact on institutions of higher education has been obvious for years. Everyone in education has

A. J. Falender and J. C. Merson (Eds.). *Management Techniques for Small and Specialized Institutions.*
New Directions for Higher Education, no. 42. San Francisco: Jossey-Bass, June 1983.

watched elementary schools close, then junior high schools, then high schools. Nevertheless, some people in higher education still want to believe that the crunch will not arrive at the college level or that alternative sources of college students will be found. Some college officials hope that the reprieve will come in the form of foreign students. Others hope to attract students from other colleges!

The hope for the foreign student market can be seen in the number of conference panels on this topic and in the substantial increase in foreign travel by admissions staff. While some colleges will increase their number of foreign students, most will have great difficulty competing in this market. First, the number of foreign students who possess the educational skills and financial resources needed to attend an American college is limited. Recruiting foreign students who need full scholarships and remedial programs will not solve a college's financial problems. Second, the colleges that are succeeding in this market have developed extensive recruitment programs to attract foreign students. Many of these colleges have also developed intensive support programs for these students once they arrive on campus. In any case, before admissions staff invest thousand of dollars in competing for foreign students, they should obtain a copy of *Open Doors* (Boyan, 1981), a book that provides information on the countries from which students come, the universities that they have historically attended, and the academic majors that they select. After reading this book, one can better evaluate a college's position in this competitive market.

It will also be extremely difficult for a college to enter new domestic geographic markets during this decade. First, 93 percent of entering freshmen attend a college within 500 miles of their home. Second, to enter a new geographic market takes a concerted effort involving admissions staff, alumni, and other expensive resources. A college should know why it will be competitively stronger in the new market than the college of comparable quality that is already well entrenched in that market. Thus, few colleges will be able to compensate for population decline in their own region by raiding students from other colleges. In fact, most colleges would do better to solidify their current market than to use their limited resources on ill-considered expansion into new markets.

The Impact

There are two models for allocating the impact of declining student enrollment. The first model is a trickle-down model. Under this model, the quality of students at almost all colleges will decline significantly during this decade. To illustrate, let us assume three rank-ordered colleges, A, B, and C, each of which enrolls a hundred students. Institution A can expect to lose thirty-three of its current quality students over the next decade to the population decline, so it lowers its standards and takes thirty-three students who would have attended institution B. B loses thirty-three students to declining population plus thirty-three students to institution A. Consequently, institution B must reach down and take sixty-six students from institution C. Institution C loses thirty-three students to the population decline and sixty-six students to institution B. The implications are clear. If you are a second-tier college, two thirds of tomorrow's students will not be enrolled today. If you are a third-tier college, none of tomorrow's students will be enrolled today. Each college must decide how to deal with the consequences of a substantial decline in the quality of its student body. Will you be able to justify the substantial cost differential between your college and public institutions without the quality level of your current student body?

The second model for allocating the declining number of students assumes that there will be a rapid and significant decline in the supply side of higher education that will allow many institutions to preserve their current quality. Under this model, certain institutions are perceived to be in trouble by students, parents, and guidance counselors. These institutions will perish in short order, since students will avoid a failing college. Thus, one third of the current colleges will lose all their students and thereby permit the surviving colleges to maintain today's standards.

Who Is Responsible?

Both models described in the preceding section assume a large number of losers. It is the task of the college president to position his or her college in the winner's column. At this point, let us fix responsibility for the survival of the institution where it belongs — on the shoulders of the president and faculty. The admissions director can only publicize the successes (or try to hide the failures) of the administration and faculty. Ask an admissions director what the most important step in recruiting a student is, and you will be told that it is to get the prospective student and parents to visit the campus. Once on campus, the prospective student will learn how the college differs from the image conveyed by its brochures. It is the administration and faculty that create the reality of the institution.

Enrollment Plan

The way out of the impasse created by declining enrollment is for the small college to manage its resources so well that it can outpace its peers and become one of the small percentage of colleges that maintain their current quality. Is it realistic to think that a small institution with a limited budget can compete with the intensive recruitment activities of large institutions? Yes, but only if well-targeted and coordinated resources are used in imaginative ways.

The best method of ensuring that the college's limited resources are well coordinated and targeted is to develop an enrollment plan. This plan should explicitly identify the institution's strengths and weaknesses. That is, it should identify the institution's competitive place in the higher education market; its resources for the future and its plans for spending them; the type of student who should come to the institution, where these students come from, how many of them exist now, and how many there will be during this decade; and what these students need to be told to interest them in the institution and what channels can be used to reach them.

Since the enrollment plan addresses the institution's overall goals, resources, and performance, it must be created under the president's direction. While the admissions dean will be a major contributor, the admissions function is only one part of the total enrollment plan. The president has overall responsibility for the plan, including obtaining the data that will permit those involved in developing the plan to understand the consequences of all proposals, confronting the painful trade-offs that will have to be made if the institution is to survive, writing the plan, getting community approval, implementing the plan, and sticking with it through the tough days.

The people who develop the enrollment plan should represent the key constituencies of the college and control its major resources. They must answer such questions as what departments should be expanded or eliminated, whether class size or admissions standards should be lowered, and what the tuition policy should be and how to pay for it. Consequently, the group that develops the enrollment plan includes the admissions dean, the academic deans, the financial vice-president, and alumni and student representatives.

The committee that develops the enrollment plan should begin by making a realistic assessment of the college. From working with colleges, I have found that such assessment will be accurate only if it is based on hard data, not on the perceptions of college faculty and administration. If self-perceptions can be credited, more than 90 percent of the colleges fall into the top 10 percent — a mathematical impossibility. Only by confronting the reality of its current market position can a college expect to do well during the remainder of this decade.

The major sources of market research information available to the small college include a report by WICHE (McConnell, 1979) that details the demographic data on college-bound population for the nation, region, states, and counties; the freshmen attitude survey conducted by the Cooperative Institutional Research Program of the American Council on Education; and data from the Educational Testing Service (ETS) of Princeton, New Jersey. The American Council on Education (ACE) can provide a college with extensive information on the attitudes of college-bound students and their parents. Three profiles are available from ACE: one of all students who enrolled at participating colleges in the preceding fall, one of the students who enrolled at participating colleges that have similar characteristics, and one of an institution's own enrolling class. These data allow an institution to assess not only the overall college-bound market but also its own specific market segment. Finally, ETS can provide an institution with extensive data on students who have requested that their test scores be sent to it. ETS can tell the institution what high schools these students attended and what other colleges the students sent their scores to. ETS can also prepare a profile comparing the class that enrolls at the institution with the group that sent the scores. Finally, when an institution provides a list of the students who completed the first year of college, ETS can compare the profile of the retained group with the profile of earlier groups.

Institutional research is another useful source of market information. A well-run admissions office should have extensive data on the characteristics of the nonapplied students (those who made inquiries but did not apply), on the nonenrolled (those who were admitted but who enrolled elsewhere), and on the enrolled. Information on how the college is perceived by prospective applicants, parents, guidance directors, current students, and alumni should be included in this analysis.

By analyzing all these data, the committee can make a brutally honest assessment of the college as it now stands and forecast the future that it can expect if no major changes are made. The attitudinal and demographic data from these sources give the committee the capability to make very precise forecasts of future enrollment at the college.

The enrollment plan should be a written document so that the decisions can be discussed campuswide. The need for those decisions must also be discussed. Unless faculty, administrators, students, and alumni understand the necessity for the proposed programs, they will not provide the support necessary for successful implementation of the programs. And, it is the support of these groups that allows the admissions office to create the personalized recruitment program that the small college needs.

Another reason for a well-thought-out enrollment plan is that new programs can have damaging unintended consequences. Recently, a financially strong and academically selective Southern regional college expanded its size and greatly increased its recruitment of Northern students. The recruitment program was highly successful. However, the new students have not blended with the others, and divisiveness on campus has been a result. The college is now in danger of losing its traditional market.

Admissions Plan

The admissions plan, one major section of the enrollment plan, should explicitly detail the programs that will promote the college, the costs of those programs, and their results. This plan forms the basis of the contract between admissions and the rest of the college and provides the performance criteria for measuring the admissions office. Naturally, the admissions dean can be held accountable for meeting the agreed upon targets only if all the other aspects of the enrollment plan are implemented on schedule.

The first priority of the admissions plan should be to develop high-quality admissions materials and a professional staff. All serious applicants will come into contact both with a college's basic materials and with admissions staff. This contact will often greatly influence their final opinion of the college. Does admissions respond promptly to requests for admissions materials so that students receive the material before they narrow their choices? Is this basic literature well designed, and does its content and style convey the basic purpose and feel of the college? Are the receptionists and admissions staff courteous and helpful so that they reinforce the institution's message of a caring, supportive academic environment? Why should a prospective student believe that faculty are accessible if admissions staff are not?

The second priority of the admissions plan should be to shore up the college's existing markets—the current feeder schools and admissions pools. Data analysis will undoubtedly indicate that a large percent of the incoming class comes from a relatively small number of high schools. Admissions staff should ensure that the institution has a favorable impression at those feeder schools and take steps to maintain that impression. Maintaining a favorable impression takes considerable effort. In the fall, when college staff are trying to identify and recruit potential applicants, they are very solicitous of high school staff. Feeder schools greatly appreciate the colleges that revisit in late spring to explain the decisions that were made on applicants. Admissions staff should remember that numerous other colleges will initiate programs to court the same feeder schools.

Another area of great potential at many colleges is the current inquiry pool—individuals who have requested literature, submitted test scores, visited the campus, or in any other way initiated contact with the college. Unusally, only 10 to 20 percent of the inquiry pool will submit applications. Therefore, even a small increase in the yield from the inquiry pool can result in substantial incrase in the applicant pool.

Innovative new programs should not be developed at the expense of basic operations. Increasingly, we hear from high school students how difficult it is to schedule an interview with a well-informed member of the admissions board. Why? Often, it is because admissions staff are developing massive direct mail campaigns and other programs that will serve only to bring even more students into contact with a nonresponsive admissions office.

A college's current students have the greatest credibility with and access to prospective students. Properly used, they can become a low-cost high-quality sales force for the college. For example, each fall, Wesleyan College in Connecticut asks its 650 freshmen to identify students in their former high school who would be strong candidates for admission. To these students, Wesleyan sends admissions materials and a letter stating that a current student names them as a promising candidate for admission. Eighty percent of these prospects—a total of 240 students—will apply to Wesleyan. Thus, the Wesleyan program may well be the most cost-effective recruiting program in the country.

Student holidays—Thanksgiving, Christmas, and spring break—occur at good times in the admissions cycle to allow students to contact prospects, former teachers, and guidance staff from their home town. And these trips cost the college nothing in travel funds. In some situations, current students will have better access to former high school teachers and guidance staff than admissions staff will have. Due to budget cuts, staff at the larger suburban feeder high schools is being reduced. At the same time, an increasing number of colleges are trying to develop relationships with those schools. Consequently, the admissions representative may have contact only with the guidance office secretary. However, a well-liked former student who returns will have easy access to a former adviser. Nevertheless, there are limits on the use of students. High school staff enjoy hearing a student's impression of the college, but they do not want to discuss admissions requirements or special situations with current college students or alumni representatives.

Conclusion

The next five years will be very difficult from an admissions perspective. To survive, a college must have both a president and an admissions director who realize, first, that not enough students will go on to college in the next decade to support today's colleges at their present levels of quantity and quality; second, that no programs will create the students needed to maintain the existing levels; third, that a college will have to outperform its peer institutions if it is to survive; fourth, that admissions is an institutional function that is only coordinated by the dean of admissions; and, fifth, that even the most talented admissions director cannot succeed without the active support of the president and faculty.

References

Boyan, D. R. (Ed.) *Open Doors: 1980–81.* New York: Institute for International Education, 1981.
McConnell, W. R. *High School Graduates: Projections for the Fifty States.* Boulder, Colo.: Western Interstate Commission on Higher Education, 1979.

Carl Allen is president of Preview Inc., an admissions consulting firm that specializes in strategy planning and audiovisual presentations.

When a new reality is in place to support it, the school's image can be changed through systematic efforts to communicate with key constituents.

The Public Image of a Small College

Rosemary Ashby

The public image of a small college has a persistent life of its own, however unlike the current reality it may be. Old images die hard, but they can be refashioned. With time and hard work, a college can project a new image that will break through the hearsay and opinion that build up over the years and greatly enhance recruitment and fund-raising efforts. The case of Pine Manor College provides a good example of the process.

Pine Manor College is a small liberal arts college for women located in the metropolitan Boston area, along with fifty-five other institutions of higher education. It started life as an exclusive and expensive women's junior college, and over the years it accumulated various unflattering labels associated with such an origin. As a result, alumnae were often inclined to anonymity. By the early 1970s, a number of women's colleges had closed due to declining enrollments. Others, in response to the decision of many men's colleges to admit women, began to admit men. Many prospective students and their parents wondered whether Pine Manor had closed. Others, vaguely aware that it had survived, questioned the reason to be of single-sex education or the validity of the two-year experience.

The effect of our poor image on morale was insidious, especially for current students whoe tenuous allegiance to the college was constantly

A. J. Falender and J. C. Merson (Eds.). *Management Techniques for Small and Specialized Institutions.*
New Directions for Higher Education, no. 42. San Francisco: Jossey-Bass, June 1983.

threatened by negative comments about the institution that they encountered in the greater Boston area. This had serious implications for admissions. Most alumnae acknowledged that they had received a sound educational grounding at the college and that this grounding had given them access as transfer students to a wide range of senior colleges, but they were not vocal in their support for the college. Fund raising was not meeting the college's needs. Participation in alumnae giving was low, and many older alumnae seemed unaware of the college's financial needs. Foundation support was minimal, because the college was not perceived as a serious academic institution that should receive the same consideration as other colleges. In short, the college needed urgently to reestablish a national visibility and credibility. While some of these problems may have been peculiar to Pine Manor College, I think that Pine Manor's efforts to resolve them is relevant to other small colleges.

Defining the New Image

Faculty, staff, and students all agreed that Pine Manor's greatest problem was that the outside world did not perceive the quality and integrity of its academic program. As a result, the college resolved to reverse an outdated image and shape a new one. It was vital to find some key factor, a shift in direction or a change in program that could give impetus to this task of fashioning a new image. In Pine Manor's case, this key factor was a change in our charter in 1977, which permitted us to grant the bachelor of arts degree for the first time in our sixty-year history. This change provided the central focus for all the other statements that we wished to make about the college, its academic programs, and, most important, its graduates.

Led by the president, the college set out to define its mission, translate that mission into a series of concrete examples drawn from the academic program and services, and orchestrate the delivery of a coherent and consistent message to the outside world. Pine Manor agreed that its mission was to give women access to a wide range of options in the professions. The most effective strategy that we had developed combined theory with practice, classroom work with practical exposure to careers through internships. The measure of our success was the success of our graduates in the world beyond Pine Manor College.

We believed that our audience was particularly interested in the end result of a college education in these inflationary times and that its members were concerned about tangible benefits and prospects of employment. We therefore wished to present ourselves as an academic institution whose curriculum, requirements, and special services were directed at giving women the skills, knowledge, confidence, and practical experience that could give them a competitive edge in the job market. The focus included a mathematics requirement, writing skills, computer literacy, and internships that provided job experience and that often led to job placement. This was the image that we wanted to project: applied liberal arts; broad, lasting, and practical education; a competent and employable graduate. The key tools in launching the updated image were revised publications and an intensive public relations effort directed at several key constituencies: our own community, the surrounding community, and alumnae.

The Starting Point: Campus and Surrounding Community

Image building begins in one's own backyard, with faculty, staff, and current students. Then it expands to neighborhoods, sister institutions, and finally the general public. The job description that I wrote as a very green president seven years ago still stands: "In terms of external affairs, it is my goal to work with the board of trustees, the alumnae association, parents, neighbors, and both private and governmental organizations to secure and build support for the college by effectively conveying Pine Manor's educational mission and by instilling confidence in the future of the college among all constituents and potential and actual benefactors. It is important to increase the college's visibility and to secure recognition for the quality of it academic program." The best way to appear as a vital academic institution is to behave like one. The approaches are many, but all need the support of a vigorous public relations office that keeps an eye on the newsworthy. Moreover, all the approaches require the efforts of every member of the college community.

Pine Manor College moved on a number of fronts. We established a program of outstanding speakers—outstanding even for a major cultural and educational center like Boston. Our first triumph was an evening with the Irish actress, Siobhan McKenna, who performed work by James Joyce. More than 1,100 people attended the event. For many, it was their first visit to the campus. If one can be judged by the company that one keeps, these people came away with an impression that was extremely favorable to the college. The event received major coverage in the media. Since that day, the roster of speakers who have appeared on campus in support of each of our B.A. programs has been truly outstanding. The president needs to exploit every contact open to the college through trustees, parents, and alumnae to ensure the presence of vital and stimulating visitors to the campus. Invitations for these evenings are always sent to local high school guidance counselors and teachers, faculty from other colleges, local alumnae, and neighbors.

We encouraged faculty and staff to be visible in professional associations and meetings, to present papers, and to serve on panels on topics ranging from programs for international students to single-sex education and study skills. This visibility helped to establish the image of Pine Manor as a dynamic institution in the vanguard. The college also sought out affiliations with local professional organizations in areas as diverse as infant development and the decorative arts. The college now hosts a number of professional meetings and organizations. Cross-registration, faculty exchanges, and team teaching with other colleges have also given exposure to our academic program and faculty. Athletic teams have been built up. The results of every intercollegiate match are widely listed, and no college can afford to be always in the loser column without having its image suffer. If we are listed as Pine Manor Junior College or if we are identified in a way that we feel does not present the college accurately, letters to the editor are promptly dispatched. Finally, the placement of effective student interns in organizations and businesses throughout the greater Boston area has been an enormous boost to our image locally.

The president has a key role to play in ensuring that all communications — regular correspondence, newsletters, alumnae bulletin articles, and speeches on campus at parent's weekends, at board meetings, and around the country at alumnae gatherings — highlight specific success stories that illustrate Pine Manor's strengths and enhance its image. I frequently talk about student acceptance into prestigious graduate schools, student entry into the job market, and students who have been hired by organizations that they served well as interns. The same students are called on to speak on panels for students and parents and to speak to alumnae groups. These students are superb examples of the reality that underlies the image that we are working so hard to project.

The Key Constituency: Alumnae

The place to start rebuilding a college's image outside the immediate community is with its graduates. It is essential for alumnae to be clearly identified with their college, both in their own community and to the broad public through publications. The image of an institution is established most quickly through its alumnae and their professional achievements, which include major responsibilities in volunteer work. For prospective students, alumnae embody the access to personal and professional success that the college can provide. For prospective donors, the alumnae provide a measure of the quality, focus, and effectiveness of the college's academic programs. The president of the college must travel to every part of the country to update alumnae on the college, to instill a sense of pride in their association with the college, to gather information about alumnae careers, and to enlist alumnae support in projecting a positive image of the college. As visible and vocal members of its graduate body, alumnae combine the roles of cheerleader and reporter.

As already noted, publications play a major role in this kind of outreach. In 1979, Pine Manor College revised its alumnae bulletin to focus on the achievements of alumnae in a wide range of professional fields. We began with the performing arts, featuring, among others, an Emmy award–winning television news producer, two nationally known film actresses, a principal singer with the New York City Opera, a documentary filmmaker, and a script writer. The response from alumnae was enormous.

Slowly, an image of the strong, competent, and talented Pine Manor graduate began to take hold. This proved to be the first step in motivating hitherto anonymous alumnae to reclaim the college as their own and in encouraging them to be identified with it. The effect on both internal morale and external perceptions of the college was immediate. At the same time, admissions publications were redesigned to include profiles of alumnae in the professions that established the link between professional success and the years spent at the college.

The second step was to bring alumnae back to the college as distinguished visiting alumnae to speak in classes, exhibit their work, serve on panels, and lecture to the college and surrounding community. Whenever possible, interviews with local media were arranged, and there was always coverage by internal publications. An alumnae career data bank was established to allow us to locate alumnae in a wide range of fields. There is now widespread recognition on campus of the enormous number of success stories among Pine Manor graduates. There is a growing sense of pride in the institution among students, parents, and alumnae as they hear, meet, or read about the American editor of French *Vogue* and *Vogue Hommes,* the staff writer for the *Los Angeles Herald Examiner* who was nominated for a Pulitzer prize, or the vice-president of a major Wall Street brokerage house.

The president is in a key position to set the whole process in motion. It is essential for the president to be able to project a strong image of the college to alumnae in the field and to collect and disseminate the wealth of information that will round out that image with specific detail. An eye for fitting each small part of a complex picture into place is important. In the last analysis, that is what brings the image to life. The sense of continuity that the president can give to the image of the college is also important. New developments can be presented as evolutions of old hallmarks, not as overnight changes. At Pine Manor College, for example, the internship program is not too distant from the concept of the practice house, which flourished for many years at the college as the practical component of the homemaking program. Like it or not, the president is the college to many of its constituents, and he or she must be able to reflect its strengths, aspirations, successes, and needs.

Image and Recruitment

The image of a college is vital to success in admissions. The first contact that a prospective student has with the college will most often be through admissions publications. As already noted, Pine Manor College has worked hard to project a new image through this medium, one that stresses the role of the college giving students knowledge, skills, and practical experience and that illustrates graduates' successes in the job market. At the same time, we set up regional organizations in key admissions areas where there were substantial numbers of alumnae who could be called on to contact prospective students and organize events at which current students and parents could meet with prospective students consumer to consumer. Current students who spoke about their Pine Manor experience to local alumnae, prospective students and their parents, and local guidance counselors at such events as an annual Christmas luncheon had an immediate impact on the image of the institution. We also communicated with students and parents throughout the admissions year about activities on campus, building projects, gifts and grants, and honors and awards to faculty. Keeping channels of communication open with current parents and constantly reinforcing a positive image are important factors in retention. Finally, we were fortunate enough to find a trustee to underwrite a program that brought high school guidance counselors from key areas to the campus for a two-day visit so that reality could displace an outworn image.

Image and Fund Raising

Image problems are generally more acute among small, less prestigious colleges. It is exactly this group that has the hardest time establishing credibility with both major donors and foundations. The major donors tend to think of the small institution in small terms. Many foundations seem to feel that they are on safer ground if they give to major institutions than if they move into unknown territory by funding a college that is less traditional and therefore less serious, less substantive, and more high-risk.

In working with both individuals and foundations, the president's first task is to establish that the college serves a distinct category of students whose needs have a legitimate claim on outside support. The president must also make a strong case for the mission of the college. For Pine Manor College, we made the case for the student with an average record who could be expected to establish a solid record of achievement by means of the college's programs and services. While our graduates are not dissimilar from those of more competitive and prestigious colleges, our entering freshmen are very different — they have enormous potential, but they often do not excel in conventional testing situations. We feel that this type of student and the college that serves her deserve support. The president needs a strong data base at this stage, because the college must be able to document where its students begin, where they go on to graduate school, who hires them, and how they perform.

Nothing succeeds like success. When the first breakthrough is made and a major foundation recognizes that the small college has a deserving case and funds its proposal, there is an immediate effect on the image of the institution and on its donor ranks. The first grant is immensely helpful in establishing credibility for the college, and publicizing the grant can bring great dividends. It is also essential to report faithfully to all donors on the concrete progress that their funds have made possible. Such reporting brings renewed support to the institution, since it establishes its image as an effective, well-run organization that serves a specific constituency.

In proposing projects for funding and in submitting supporting documentation, colleges should be alert to the opportunities for image building. Pine Manor's first small but very significant grant from a major foundation came in support of a proposal to fund the development of writing courses in which students would do all their writing and editing on computer terminals. The project itself reflected the institution's commitment to good writing skills, to familiarizing women with technology, and to giving women a competitive edge in the job market. The image reflected in the project was positive. Second, we had good supporting evidence of the success record of our graduates in the professional world. Third, we tackled what might appear to be negatives — our students' average College Board scores, for instance — in an affirmative way.

Conclusion

Image building is a circular process. Awareness of the need to project a strong image leads an institution to take a hard look at the realities of its programs and services and to make changes that strengthen the college at every level. This in turn enhances the college's image, which reflects an improved reality. It is perhaps establishing the stronger image that is the more complex process. Every promotional avenue must be explored, and every channel of communication must be used to publicize a coherent, consistent record of success and service to a distinct population. Building a sense of institutional pride and involving all constituencies in the documentation and broadcasting of the institution's record are essential. The president must orchestrate and conduct this group performance, selecting the theme, setting the tone, and designating the audience. Once we realize that images are not immutable, we can look at everything differently. At my particular college, a full house, a balanced budget, a successul capital campaign, an annual fund that doubled over three years, and a great increase in favorable publicity all testify to the rewards of tackling the task of changing one's image. Most important of all, the students are noticeably prouder of their institution, and both students and alumnae have become vocal supporters of its program.

Rosemary Ashby has been president of Pine Manor College since 1976.

Managing our colleges during a period of decline requires strong leadership. Organizing the search process to find such leaders means striking a balance between structure and flexibility.

Searching for Senior Administrators

James M. Unglaube

For most of the history of this nation, enrollment in colleges and universities continued to grow with only minor interruptions. Between 1963 and 1975, the growth was phenomenal, more than doubling from just under 5 million to more than 11 million. However, enrollment has grown very little since 1975, and in two of those years it actually declined. The present decline in the traditional college-age population will have a dramatic effect on most institutions of higher education. At the same time, the national and the international economy have had a severe impact on American colleges and universities. In such a context, the role of administrative leadership is critical. The times make high-quality presidential and vice-presidential leadership absolutely necessary in higher education. How are colleges to identify and select the kinds of leaders who will be able to face the challenges of these times aɪ ⹂lead their institutions in the 1980s and 1990s? This chapter focuses on the search process for presidential leadership, and it touches on the search for institutional vice-presidents.

The President

Every year, hundreds of institutions of higher education face the prospect of selecting a president. According to Nason (1980), the selection of a

A. J. Falender and J. C. Merson (Eds.). *Management Techniques for Small and Specialized Institutions.*
New Directions for Higher Education, no. 42. San Francisco: Jossey-Bass, June 1983.

new president is the most important responsibility of a board of trustees. If the task is important, then it is imperative that it be done well. However, most boards of trustees are not prepared for the task of conducting a search and making a selection, and many trustees have never experienced the process. If the search process is done well, the investment that it requires can pay dividends well into the future. The next three sections deal with the presidential search process: organizing the search, conducting the search, and selecting the new president.

Organizing the Search

The search process begins with an announcement by the incumbent president that he or she is resigning or with a vacancy created by illness or death. Frequently, the board of trustees or its leadership has advance information on the impending vacancy. An important consideration is to whom the resignation is directed and when or where it is announced. The president is responsible to the board of trustees, and ultimately the board must receive and accept the resignation. The board of trustees will also establish the procedure by which a new president will be selected. If the resignation is not announced at a meeting of the board, it is advisable for the entire board to meet as soon as possible. If the board leadership has advance notice of the resignation, it may wish to prepare a recommended search process for approval by the full board.

The board of trustees has the task of structuring a search process that will lead to selection of a new president. In describing this task, Bolman (1970) indicates that knowing the institution and knowing the role of the president are both extremely important. Since the trustees are looking to match a person with an institution, they must know both the institution and the position that they wish to fill. As the board develops a search process, its members will need to deal with a number of issues: the size and composition of the search committee, the job description of the president, criteria for the position, an institutional profile, a budget, a timetable, the possible selection of an acting president, use of consultative services, and the charge to the search committee.

In developing the search process, the board of trustees will need to establish a search committee. In most colleges and universities, this committee is broadly representative, since it generally includes representatives of trustees, faculty, students, and alumni. The college administration and the local community can also be included. A good rule of thumb is for the committee to number between seven and ten members, with trustees representing a majority and providing the chairperson; frequently, the chairperson of the search committee is the chairperson of the board. It is well to ask the appropriate faculty, student, alumni, and administrative groups to select their own representative. It is important to remember that the board of trustees carries the responsibility for selecting a new president.

The trustees should also consider the job description for the presidency, the criteria for the position, and a profile of the institution. The presidential selection process is a two-way street. The institution needs to become thoroughly familiar with the final candidates, and the final candidates need to understand both the position and the institution. If a search committee advertises the position and receives nominations and applications without having first prepared a job description, criteria for the position, and an institutional profile, its members cannot answer prospective candidates' questions.

When the search committee begins its work, it should have a clear sense of the financial resources available to conduct the search. Considerable costs are involved. A search covering several months and involving interviews at more than one level can easily cost between $15,000 and $25,000. For example, a recent presidential search conducted by a midwestern liberal arts college cost $20,000. This figure includes candidates' travel costs for seven screening interviews and three final interviews with spouses, search committee costs, and secretarial services. Additional visits to the campus of the new president and moving costs added another $5,000. Sufficient funding should be made available. It will be money well spent.

A proposed timetable for the search committee is presented later in this chapter. At this point, it will suffice to say that the board of trustees needs to consider a goal for completion of the search. That goal should be realistic. Reality suggests that at least nine months should be allowed. This time can be shortened by reducing the time for gathering and reviewing credentials and interviewing candidates, but so doing can increase the chances for error. Consideration of a goal is important at this point in the event that an acting president will have to be appointed. If the incumbent president will leave before the search can be completed, it will be necessary to appoint an acting president. There are many possibilities when such an appointment is contemplated. There are also some pitfalls to avoid. Vice-presidential-level staff at the college are prime candidates. However, an acting president should never be appointed from the ranks of those seeking the position permanently. A trustee or a retired person with administrative capabilities are other possibilities.

The institution can employ the services of consultants in the search process. The Presidential Search Consultation Service, a nonprofit enterprise sponsored by the Association of American Colleges and the Association of Governing Boards of Universities and Colleges, publishes a brochure describing its services. For colleges related to a church body, the higher education office of the church body commonly offers consultative services. Other associations of institutions may do likewise. In addition, printed sources (Kauffman, 1974; Nason, 1980) can serve an instructive role in the search process. When a vacancy occurs in the presidency at a college associated with the Lutheran Church in America, the church body office immediately sends a copy of Nason (1980) to the board chairperson and offers the services of the church body executive as the search process is organized.

Finally, the board of trustees needs to issue a charge to the search committee. The charge answers questions about committee responsibilities. Will the committee narrow the pool of candidates to a single person that it will recommend to the board? Will the committee present the board with several names? If so, will the candidates be rank-ordered? Will the search committee present a small group of candidates to a selection committee that will carry out final interviews? The charge should make the task of the search committee very clear.

Conducting the Search

We have now reached the point where the search committee meets for the first time. As it gathers, it should have a clear sense of its charge from the board of trustees, a job description, criteria for the position, and a profile of the institution. While the board of trustees should approve the criteria for the position, it may be advisable for the search committee to be involved in developing them. The committee needs to deal first with a number of procedural matters: confidentiality, the search committee office, search committee staff, the application format, and the rating scale for evaluating candidates.

Confidentiality is critical to the search process. Final candidates may be subject to public identification, but the process should be kept confidential up until that point unless law dictates otherwise. The committee does need to report to its constituents on its progress. The task of reporting should be assigned to a single person, either the chairperson of the committee or to a member of the committee staff. The reporting is best done at key points along the way: when all applications and nominations are in hand and when the two interview stages have begun.

The best way to maintain confidentiality and some distance in carrying out the search is to establish an off-campus office and mailing address. That office can be the business office of the committee chairperson, and the mailing address can be that of the office or a post office box. Secretarial services are a necessity, and money should be set aside to support them. If a campus office is used for the search committee, care should be exercised both in the handling of mail and in the provision of secretarial services. If the chairperson of the search committee cannot give significant time to the process, it is a good idea to hire a part-time staff person.

The matter of what kinds of information candidates will be asked to provide should be clarified before the vacancy is announced. Many institutions develop a biographical form for use by all candidates. Such forms obviate great differences in the kinds of credentials submitted. The forms generally include a list of significant achievements (honors, awards, publications, civic activities, memberships), and personal references (not letters of reference or requests for such letters). Many institutions also request philosophical statements, personal assessments, and statements of interest in the position. Relative uniformity in the credentials supplied by candidates makes the screening process easier and the treatment of candidates fairer. The committee will be engaged in judging the relative qualifications of a hundred candidates or more. It is well for the committee to use the criteria established for the position to develop a rating scale for judging these candidates.

As the committee begins its work, a realistic timetable should be established. The length of time that it takes to complete the task may be dictated by an expectation of a report by the board of trustees or by the anticipated departure date of the incumbent president. However, the task is too important to be forced into an artificially restricted period of time. Figure 1 displays a reasonable timetable for the selection process.

Let us assume that the presidential search process has reached the point where the vacancy has been announced to the public and nominations and applications have been invited. The announcement and its placement should be sensitive to nondiscriminatory employment practices. It is possible to satisfy the need for making a national announcement to the higher education community by placing an advertisement in the *Chronicle of Higher Education,* a highly respected and widely read weekly publication that includes a bulletin board of available positions. The advertisement should appear at least twice. If the position includes any restrictions, such as religious requirements, they should be specified.

The search committee should announce the position to the various college constituent groups: faculty, students, alumni, administrators, and trustees. Higher education leaders in the state or region and leaders of consortia can also be helpful in identifying candidates. If the college is church-related, the announcement should be sent to church leaders. A realistic deadline for nominations and applications is sixty days after the vacancy has been announced.

Figure 1. A Timetable for the Selection Process

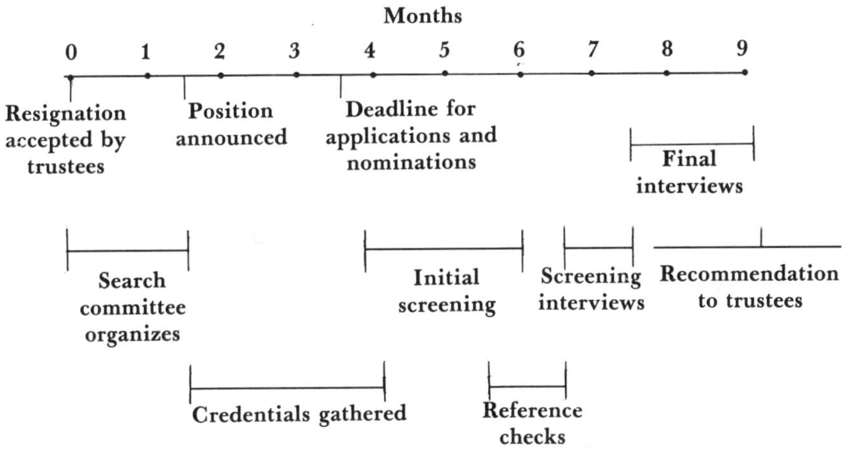

Two questions with which the committee should deal early on involve its own stance in seeking out candidates and the matter of reluctant candidates. Certain potential candidates may not wish to identify themselves with the search process. These persons may be quite successful and happy in their present position. The committee itself may wish to do some research to identify such persons as presidents of other colleges, leading educators, and church body leaders. As Fouts (1977, p. 7) says, "Many exceptionally well-qualified prospects may be unwilling to respond... either because they are satisfied with their present position, wish to avoid premature publicity, or simply are not aware of the advantages of the new position."

The process has now reached the point of examining the credentials of candidates and of beginning the initial screening. Depending on the nature of the position and the institution and any special requirements stated in the announcement, the search committee will identify somewhere between 50 and 250 candidates. It will have to be decided whether the entire committee will read all the credentials. If the number of candidates is large, the committee may wish to work in small groups and present group recommendations to the committee as a whole. To speed the review process, it may be well to distribute credentials to the committee members as they are received. Letters of reference are not necessary for this screening. This step should serve to reduce the list of candidates to twenty-five or fewer.

For this smaller list of candidates, personal letters of reference should be requested. It would be well to include a copy of the criteria for the position with the request. The committee may wish to contact references by telephone instead of or in addition to contacting them by letter. If references are contacted by telephone, the caller should work from a set of questions. A conference call involving more than one member of the search committee is a possibility. A word of warning and advice is appropriate here. Most candidates will provide references who are likely to supply very positive information. For this reason, the committee may also wish to contact other persons who are familiar with the candidate's work. Of course, the search committee must take care not to breach confidentiality, which may be important to the candidate. This advice is particularly relevant for candidates unknown to the search committee. Candidates known to the committee are more likely to have both their positive and negative characteristics known. Care should be exercised in treating these two kinds of candidates evenhandedly. Once references have been checked, the committee can narrow the list to a number ranging between five and fifteen.

Now we reach the face-to-face interview stage. Up to this point, the search committee has dealt with candidates only on paper. Since few of the candidates are likely to be known to the committee, the use of screening interviews enables committee members to meet candidates before narrowing the list down. It is advisable for the entire committee to meet at a central point easily accessible by air. Candidates can be scheduled for sixty to ninety minute interviews over a two-day period. In preparation for these interviews, candidates should receive basic information about the institution and the community. The committee should agree on an interview format. The same key questions must be raised with each candidate. Once these interviews have been completed, the committee can narrow the field to a final group, which will be interviewed again or passed along to a selection committee.

How screening interviews can best be conducted varies with circumstances. If candidates are spread across the country and their number is sizable, the search committee can split up into smaller units and conduct interviews in several cities. This procedure requires committee members to reach an understanding on how the results of these interviews will be represented to the entire committee. Some institutions have conducted one-hour interviews in a meeting room at an airport terminal. This method allows convenient scheduling for candidates and results in very little lost time for committee members. Other methods are less expeditious. One institution scheduled interviews at a location some distance from the airport in the community where the college was located. The candidates were asked to rent an automobile, drive to the town, find the motel for the night's lodging, and find the site for the interview. Being alone in the town where the college is located can embarrass the candidate who wishes to see the campus and meet people. Leaving candidates on their own does not promote a positive impression of the institution. Kauffman (1974, p. 47) addresses this issue well: "Those candidates who have survived the screening process to this point and still seek the position should be treated with the utmost personal consideration, for the final stage can be one of great delicacy. Desirable candidates may withdraw if they are not treated properly by the committee or by board members. The top persons on the list may need to be sold on the opportunity of this particular presidency." This thought has equal application for both screening and final interviews. Search committee members need to remember the dual nature of the search process: Not only are they judging candidates, they also are selling the institution. Commenting on the search process, Weaver and Farnham (1977, p. 322) have written: "An academic search committee . . . must sell the position to first-rate candidates while simultaneously judging them. These two sides of a search are so inextricably intertwined that isolating one aspect immediately distorts the whole process."

The final group of candidates, probably numbering between three and five, needs to be involved in in-depth final interviews. These interviews will be conducted by the search committee, the selection committee, or the board of trustees, depending on the structure of the search process. The interviews should include a significant period of time on campus for formal and informal meetings with members of the campus community. The reactions of the campus community should be made available to the group that conducts the interviews. If the candidate is married, the spouse should participate in the interview. Little has been said here about the spouse as that issue relates to the selection of a new president. Boards of trustees need to exercise caution in making asumptions about the involvement of the president's spouse in the life of the institution. Greater numbers of women are now being considered and employed as college presidents. Spouses, male or female, have their own careers to pursue.

Detailed information on the college needs to be shared with candidates, particularly in the financial area. The group that conducts the interviews should set a block of time aside to interview each candidate. The chairperson of the committee or the chair of the board of trustees should spend time alone with the candidate outlining such details of the presidential appointment as salary, housing, and insurance.

Making the Selection

The time has now arrived for the board of trustees to receive and consider a recommendation to select a new president. The structure of the search process will dictate the nature of the recommendation. It may be limited to a single name or it may include several names, which are either ranked or unranked. Depending on the level of their involvement in the search process. the board may choose to interview the candidates again. In any event, the search and selection process has now reached the point of selection. No one can substitute for the board's responsibility here. Once the decision has been made, it should be announced on campus before it is released to the news media.

The Vice-Presidents

Small colleges generally recruit vice-presidential leadership in four administrative areas: student personnel services, academic affairs, financial affairs, and development. The four vice-presidents, along with the new president, comprise the institution's administrative team. How does one go about filling these positions? The procedure varies with the position. In these days of shared governance on campus, student personnel and chief academic officers are generally selected through search procedures not unlike those used in selecting presidents. Financial affairs and development officers are more likely to be selected by the president in consultation with a limited number of colleagues, particularly the other vice-presidents. When any of these positions becomes vacant, it should be announced wherever candidates are likely to be identified. The *Chronicle of Higher Education* is the best national publication for such announcements. Other institutions with which the college is related should also be alerted. Frequently, vice-presidential-level positions are filled by second-level persons in the same office on the home campus or at other institutions.

A search committee for a vice-president is structured by and receives its charge from the president of the institution. The president may wish to be a part of the committee or even to chair it. If he or she does not, it is a good practice to structure the process so that the names of several candidates are forwarded to the president for a final decision. The important point is who makes the decision. If the president is to bear responsibility for the final choice, the president should remain in control of the process. Members of the search committee should include faculty and students and perhaps another administrator in addition to the president.

Resources external to the institution can be helpful in selecting vice-presidents. The Presidential Search Consultation Service is available to aid in their institutions search for academic vice-presidents. National professional organizations can also be helpful. Bolman's (1970) two rules regarding the selection of a president are applicable here also—know the institution, know the role of the position that is to be filled—if the credentials of applicants are judged against these rules, the institution is much more likely to make a good match in selecting vice-presidential leadership.

Conclusion

Pattillo (1973), p. 8) makes an important point that should not be forgotten in the search for college administrative leadership: "There is no God-given prototype for the successful college president. I once knew an effective president who was psychologically unable to make a public speech... another... who never went to college himself... a third whose administrative style was that of an absent-minded professor... [another] never taught a class in his life... [another] was quarrelsome and financially irresponsible. Each..., however, was able to define a valid mission for the institution... and gain the cooperation of colleagues and supporters who could make the dreams come true. That, in the final analysis, is the indispensable presidential attribute toward which the whole selection process is directed." That is, the desired outcome of any search for administrative leadership is to find the right person for the institution at that point in its history. This fact should never be lost sight of among the procedures necessary today for search processes.

Nason (1980) issues two final words of caution that every board of trustees should keep in mind in the search and selection process. These words are spoken to the presidential search and selection process, but they have equal validity as the president seeks to fill vice-presidential vacancies: "First, there is no single and ideal search and selection process. The best procedure will be one adapted to the nature of the institution and its particular circumstances.... Second, there is no such thing as the ideal college or university president. The differing needs of different institutions and the complex demands made of the president require different people with often quite different skills and qualities. No one possesses them all.... The important thing is the fit between the individual and the institution."

58

References

Bolman, F. D. "How Will You Find a College President?" *AGB Reports,* 1970, 12 (7).

Fouts, D. E. "Picking a President the Business Way." *AGB Reports,* 1977, *19* (1).

Kauffman, J. E. *The Selection of College and University Presidents.* Washington, D.C.: Association of American Colleges, 1974.

Nason, J. W. *Presidential Search: A Guide to the Process of Selecting and Appointing College and University Presidents.* Washington, D.C.: Association of Governing Boards of Universities and Colleges, 1980.

Pattillo, M. J. "How to Choose a College President." *ABG Reports,* 1973, *15* (5).

Weaver, S. F., and Farnham, L. J. "A Commentary on 'Selecting Academic Administrators." *Educational Record,* 1977, *58* (3).

James M. Unglaube, former academic dean at Lenoir-Rhyne College in North Carolina, is director of higher education for the Lutheran Church in America.

Small institutions can make a virtue of the necessity to use administrative staff flexibly and to train young staff.

Organizing and Staffing a Small College

Adele Simmons

Organizing charts from a range of small colleges demonstrate clearly that no single pattern describes every institution. At the same time, it is clear that the challenges facing senior management at most small colleges — as well as the tensions that surround major policy and management decisions — are similar. While this chapter is based on principles that I found to be important in developing a management structure at Hampshire College, conversations with colleagues suggest that my experience is not unusual and that my conclusions are neither new nor startling. Thus, they may enable readers to look at their own institution, add new perspectives, and raise some new questions. This chapter is based on an assumption that I wish I could change: Most small colleges have limited resources and high fixed costs. It would be wonderful if I could wax eloquent about an ideal form of organization and an ideal level of staffing that would enable us to meet all our goals within a sixty-hour workweek, but the resulting chapter would not be relevant.

We all are trying to ensure that the largest proportion of our limited resources is reserved for faculty and the academic program. Thus, when we turn to the organization and staffing of a small college, we have to focus on ways of getting a maximum return for a minimum investment. What larger institutions consider to be essential is often for us a luxury that must be eliminated. These are key questions with which we must struggle: What level

A. J. Falender and J. C. Merson (Eds.). *Management Techniques for Small and Specialized Institutions.*
New Directions for Higher Education, no. 42. San Francisco: Jossey-Bass, June 1983.

of administrative support is essential to keep the college healthy and vital? What level is so modest that senior management does not have the opportunity to ask basic strategic planning questions? What level is excessive, particularly when compared with resources available for the academic program and other support areas? While there is no one right answer for all colleges, these questions do have to be asked every year of senior officers and academic leaders. At Hampshire College, these questions are asked of a committee composed of faculty, students, and administrators that we call the Budget and Priorities Committee. The same questions are asked of senior officers and academic deans who meet as a group twice a year and of members of the trustee finance committee.

The small-college president is generally away from campus between one third and one half of the time. Thus, day-to-day management of the college must be placed in the hands of senior officers, and the president must delegate substantial authority to them. These senior officers must command the respect not only of the president but of the college community with whom they deal on a regular basis.

Among its senior officers, virtually every college includes a chief academic officer, whom I shall call the dean of faculty; a chief financial officer, whom I shall call the treasurer; and a chief development officer, whose titles have lengthened, seemingly in an effort to disguise the fact that his or her job is to try to raise money.

Five other principal areas need oversight by senior officers and direct and regular involvement by the president: general administration, which includes personnel and the physical plant; admissions; the library; long-range planning; and student affairs. On many campuses, one or more of these officers—but not all—report directly to the president. The reporting relationships vary according to the particular interests of the senior officers in place and the priority that each responsibility receives at any one point. For example, the admissions officer at Hampshire has reported to the president, to the vice-president for planning and resources, and to the dean of faculty, all within the past six years. These shifts reflect both the evolving interests of the people who have held the different supervisory jobs and a changing view of the role of admissions within the college framework.

Reporting relationships can also change to reflect shifts in the priorities of senior officers. When it became apparent that I was going to spend an increasing amount of time traveling, for example, the reporting relationship of the library was shifted from the president to the dean of faculty. Whatever the formal reporting relationships, personal relationships among senior officers are important. Neither distance nor formal structures are acceptable. Collegiality is essential. People at all levels must be willing and able to take on a variety of tasks in a small college. It is essential both for senior officers to complement one another in terms of style and interest and for tasks that several different officers can do to be clearly allocated. Hampshire's treasurer came to the college after twenty years of service as Amherst's town manager, and he has assumed virtually all responsibility for relations with the local community. This responsibility could as easily have been handled by the chief development officer or the president, depending on the nature of the problem and on the people, but it is a job that must be done, and it should be done by the person who most enjoys it.

It is essential for at least three of the top five senior officers to be articulate public spokesmen for the college. This is essential to support the college's general public relations effort, and it is an asset in trustee meetings. There are many able administrators whose strength does not lie in articulating the broad visions of the college clearly, concisely, and persuasively or in setting out options and decisions that trustees have to make. In building a team, the president must have some well-placed senior officers who have a public presence. Furthermore, one senior officer should be familiar with data analysis and data processing. Knowing what questions to ask, knowing how to collect information in the most useful and effective way, and knowing how to use that information are all extremely important.

It is easy to talk about hiring people whose skills are complementary, but it is not always easy to implement such talk, since senior officers are not all hired at the same time. When one loses a chief academic officer who is also the person most skilled in the area of data analysis, one has to decide whether to insist that the next academic officer possess the same quality or to pick someone who is clearly qualified for the job and hope that the data analysis can be done by another person hired in a turnover.

Since the president is away from campus a great deal of the time, senior staff serve as major interpreters of the campus to the president. Informal weekly staff meetings are an excellent way of ensuring that each office knows what is of concern to the others, of reaching consensus on matters of collegewide importance and on matters that have budgetary implications, and of bringing the president up to date about happenings on campus. Senior officers serve an important role as intelligence gatherers for the president and share principal responsibility for ensuring that the president is not caught by surprise. However exhausted the president may be after a long trip, it is still better to learn what is really happening on campus than to receive some polished or censored version. Senior officers must be able to sift the important from the unimportant and identify emerging problems so that they can be dealt with before they become crises. Senior officers also interpret the president to the campus. Thus, senior officers and the president's office staff can create a sense that the president is accessible and concerned or that the president is unavailable and aloof. These people, as much as the president, create the president's image.

Students come to a small college precisely because it is small. They expect to have access to virtually everyone, and they expect their problems to be dealt with seriously, promptly, and effectively, Yet, most presidents do not — and cannot — meet all their students' expectations. One of our tasks is to try to ensure that students have realistic expectations about the level of special personal care that they will receive. Another is to invent new ways of meeting their very high expectations.

Small colleges rely on middle managers for their effectiveness. Many of these people run a one-person office: a financial aid office, a career services office, a housing office, and so forth. Their supervisors are often busy, so these administrators must be independently motivated and enjoy working on their own. They need to know how and when to try out new ideas, and they must have the imagination to consider new ways of doing things. Many of these jobs are lonely. People who have an ability to take the initiative, who want responsibility, and who are willing to work in a fair amount of isolation are most effective in such one-person offices.

Moreover, everyone is such situations has to be willing on any given day to take on tasks that have very little to do with his or her own office. Invariably, an important graduate will drop in on the director of the one-person alumni affairs office while he or she is off campus. The next available person will be called on to look after that graduate — whether this person is the director of career services, the director of admissions, the director of public relations, or the head of the annual fund. When the dean of student affairs is away and a student arrives in the administration building in the middle of a breakdown, a secretary cannot say, "Helping you with your problem is not a part of my job description," and when the regular coffee maker (usually still a secretary) is out of the office, an administrator cannot say that making coffee is not part of his or her job description. Small colleges are effective when people are willing to take on an enormous range of responsibilities and tasks, regardless of the position for which they were originally hired. Moreover, they must do so with good cheer, if not with enthusiasm. Rigid job descriptions and working to rule are not a part of the small college vocabulary.

The kind of flexibility that a small college requires can have its advantages. The bureaucracy is less rigid and work relationships are not as clearly stratified, so it is possible to define and redefine jobs to suit the personal interests of the people who hold them and to respond to their needs for professional growth and development. Each year, job vacancies should be reviewed to see whether jobs can be redefined, combined, or eliminated. Often, the ways in which these redefinitions, combinations, or eliminations take place have little to do with what their titles suggest and much to do with the personal characteristics of the people who are available. Hampshire's director of planning is situated in the dean of faculty's office, not so much because of administrative logic but because the associate dean of faculty who was responsible for academic programs became increasingly interested in questions of long-range financial planning. He began doing the job in an ad hoc way, and people in the college began to look to him for answers. As financial planning and enrollment became increasingly intertwined and as this associate dean of faculty — planner developed an increasing interest in the admissions office, responsibility for that office also fell to him.

One way in which small colleges can save money is by hiring bright young people at low salaries and training them. Typically, these people leave to work for wealthy institutions once they are trained. This approach to personnel management has advantages as well as disadvantages. Bright young people have lots of time and energy, but they are short on experience. When they are placed in a fairly autonomous situation, the opportunity for mistakes can be substantial. At the same time, their imagination and energy can benefit the college enormously. Moreover, the price of a mistake is not always so costly. Young people, if mismatched for one job, can more easily move on to another job than someone who has been brought in at a middle or senior level. Of course, it is in the interest of the college to find ways of keeping some of the best young people — one of whose responsibilities can be to train and work with new groups of young people. Their career development can become a central concern of the president. Often, able young people can learn new skills and continue to serve the college in a variety of ways.

In a small college, rumors circulate rapidly. Since secrets cannot be kept, it is best to adopt an open style and to develop mechanisms for communicating regularly with all constituencies. Moreover, the communication must go both ways. Bright young middle managers have ideas, and they want to be heard. They also want to know what is going on.

One considerable source of tension for small colleges is the extent to which personnel matters are handled on the strength of individual cases or on the basis of policy. The absence of policy in a given area means that the college has a great deal of flexibility in responding to individual situations in a way that meets the needs of the person in difficulty. However, the absence of policy can also create a sense of inequity among other employees. Hampshire has never had a formal sick leave policy. Individual employees have worked out sick leaves with their supervisor and the personnel office in a way that we like to believe has been extremely responsive to their needs. However, any student of organization could make a strong case that it is irresponsible not to have a sick leave policy and that we are leaving ourselves open to lawsuits from people who believe that they have been treated unfairly. I suspect that Hampshire will adopt a policy fairly soon precisely because of the legal vulnerability. But, we continue to try to establish formal policies that preserve the flexibility that enables us to treat employees as individuals. The balance that must be struck is extremely delicate.

The image left in the reader's mind by the preceding paragraphs may be one of chaos — flexibility, job descriptions revised to suit individual interests and skills, people with little experience hired to perform jobs under minimal supervision. Where is the glue? What makes the small college work under these circumstances? Several factors are essential for success. One is commitment of administrative staff to the college and its mission. Another is a sense of colleagueship, which sometimes has to be nurtured. A third criterion is formal and structured communication among officers.

Effective college administration depends on an able group of senior officers who work together, not at cross-purposes. In the midst of keeping up with day-to-day work, the president must find time for long-range planning — for developing a vision for the college in cooperation with senior officers and faculty leadership and for working to implement that plan. Only the president has the overall perspective to ensure that such planning is done. The college also depends on some basic understanding among faculty that administrative support is required to make the college work and that some kinds of decisions, for better or for worse, are administrative. If these factors are in place, a little good luck helps. Above all, a sense of humor is essential to survival.

Adele Simmons has been president of Hampshire College since 1977.

Using creative approaches and modern design and implementation techniques, a small college can successfully meet the challenge of information management in the computer age at a reasonable cost.

Computer-Supported Information Systems

William H. Mayhew

The job of every administrator is largely one of managing information. This is particularly true of institutions of higher education, partly because their interaction with governmental and private funding agencies is so broad, partly because they are so complex, but significantly because they place such a high value on information and knowledge.

The complexities of managing the various kinds of information present in a college or university are substantial, and they are largely independent of the size of the school. While large colleges and universities must deal with a greater volume of information than small colleges do, the kinds of data that both kinds of institution must maintain and the relationships among the items of information and the processing steps are quite similar. Moreover, for both kinds of institution it is important, even urgent, to maintain that information in an accurate and timely manner.

Enter the computer. Until a few years ago, only the largest organizations could afford or justify the use of computers. Now, it is clear that the era of a computer on every desk is not far off. However, the recent rapid advances in computer technology and the recent changes in computer marketing strategies have created some problems for the person who must manage an institution's overall performance. How, for instance, does one decide what kind of computer or other office automation technology is appropriate for a specific kind of problem? How does one avoid the pitfalls and potentially serious prob-

A. J. Falender and J. C. Merson (Eds.). *Management Techniques for Small and Specialized Institutions.*
New Directions for Higher Education, no. 42. San Francisco: Jossey-Bass, June 1983.

lems that can result from an incorrect choice? How does one deal with departments that are anxious to get on line but who fail to appreciate the broader implications of their individual information management activities? How does one develop a comprehensive institutionwide approach to automated information management? Indeed, is such a goal worth pursuing?

Let us examine the case of a small college that successfully faced these challenges. While the college itself is fictitious, all the situations presented in the case study actually happened in one or more organizations with which the author has been involved. This college is located in a major metropolitan area of the United States. Its superb faculty, its reputation for educational excellence, its good facilities, and its location all enable it to attract students from around the world. The student population is small, and faculty are extremely gifted and well qualified.

About a dozen years ago, the college decided to automate its bookkeeping by using an outside computer service bureau. There were a few problems, but the application was relatively straightforward, and no major design complications arose. A standard corporate accounting package was the heart of the system, which provided the information that was required, albeit in a form that typically required interpretation to staff by the business office and usually a few corrections as well.

Before long, word about the success of the business office reached other departments. The registrar was one of the first to take note, followed in short order by the development office, the admissions office, and the financial aid office. As the years went by, each department developed its own technique for using the new technology. Most departments used outside service bureaus; indeed, most departments used the same outside service bureau. However, each system was separate from the others, and whatever information had to flow between departments did so in the form of handwritten notes or specially ordered computer printouts that were expensive and somewhat hard to come by.

While all this was going on, computer technology was advancing. In the course of eight years, interactive computers became a fact, not just a fad, and it was becoming clear to every department that the service bureau approach was not without problems. The situation was probably worst in the registrar's office. First, the typical ten-day turnaround between the time when information was submitted to the company on the prescribed forms and the time when the resulting printouts were returned was too long for something like an updated class list. Second, when the list finally arrived, it always seemed to contain a few errors—not all that many, but still enough to be annoying. Time constraints meant that the errors had to be corrected by hand on the printouts, since there was no time to wait for a corrected computer run before the class list was distributed to faculty. Third, the constant flow of course adds and drops by students made it difficult to assess just who was in which course, since the data were changing so rapidly. The fact that several people worked in clerical positions in the office, including student aides, only compounded the problem. Clearly, something had to be done.

Analyzing Needs

The college decided that the time was ripe to take an organizationwide approach to information management. The administrator consulted with friends and colleagues and finally approached two consultants about conducting a needs analysis for the college that would also serve as a request for proposals (RFP) that could be submitted to vendors of computer services. The first consultant was a representative of the major accounting firm that routinely audited the college accounts and that consulted with the college on financial matters. The firm had a substantial reputation, and it could be counted on to deliver a well-packaged, impressive, and reasonably thorough report. The approach that it would advocate was likely to be conservative, but it might also be expensive. Indeed, the accounting firm requested a fee of $30,000 for the needs analysis alone.

The second consultant was an independent who had several years' experience in designing and developing information management systems for nonprofit organizations, although he had not designed such systems for colleges or universities. His package was more of a gamble. Moreover, while he has several strong references, his report would clearly not carry the same weight with the board as a report from the accounting firm. However, it also carried a much lower price tag: about $6,000.

The administrator was sufficiently interested in the project and in conserving college funds that he chose the second approach, believing that careful monitoring and supervision could help to ensure that the college got what it needed out of the study. When the study was completed in about two months' time, it was circulated to perhaps a dozen potential vendors of computer equipment, software, and related services.

Evaluating Proposals

Bidders were given about a month in which to respond. The RFP identified each department and its applications and workload. It described the problems with existing systems and the goals for new systems. It identified priorities within individual departments and across the entire college arrived at by the consultant and the chief administrator. Further, the RFP identified the number of on-line terminals that would be required, the volume of transactions that would be processed, the peak processing periods, and the kinds of software systems—data base management, word processing, electronic mail, budget management—that would be needed, but it also tried to encourage respondents to be creative within the stated guidelines. The college was particularly wary of buying, staffing, and maintaining equipment—partly from fear, partly because there was no place to put it—so time-sharing and other creative approaches were suggested.

About a third of the organizations that received the RFP chose not to respond. All but two proposals from the rest were for complete hardware-software packages. Most of the proposals were submitted by teams of equipment manufacturers and software houses. No equipment manufacturer presented a complete proposal on its own. Only two proposals offered time-sharing as an alternative. The complete-system options ranged in price from about $125,000 to more than $300,000. These prices covered minicomputers, between six and twelve terminals, varying amounts of storage capacity, and all software, but they excluded the cost of college staff involvement. Some bidders said that no additional staff resources would be required; others called for adding as many as four new people to the college payroll.

One of the time-sharing proposals was submitted by a local nonprofit organization that had a substantial computer installation and that had been involved in sharing that resource with other nearby groups the past several years. The independent consultant who prepared the RFP participated in this proposal as a potential software developer. Clearly, there was a conflict of interest, but it had been recognized while the RFP was being developed, and the consultant and the administrator had worked hard to resolve it. Each point in the RFP was reviewed carefully and considered for evidence of bias; the fact that the RFP was critically acclaimed by all the bidders was evidence of some success. The proposal submitted by the nonprofit organization called for about $35,000 in software development costs, $30,000 for equipment — terminals, printers, host computer — and about $30,000 annually in computer time once the system was operating. The computer time charges were quite reasonable compared with the $100,000 that typical commercial services were apt to charge.

The other time-sharing proposal was based on central equipment that had yet to be installed and on an organization that had yet to demonstrate its ability to manage a time-sharing computer service, although the offerer had been in the traditional service bureau business for some time. The choice was easy. The cost savings were evident, along with the risks: The nonprofit organization that hosted the computer had a good reputation for sound, basic service; while not of the caliber that the commercial organizations proposed, it was probably adequate. The nonprofit organization's proposal was accepted.

Design and Implementation

The system design approach that the successful bidder employed was unique in several respects. First, the computer facility on which the work was to be undertaken was reasonably modern, with adequate capacity to handle at least the near-term (one- to two-year) requirements of the college and with the ability to upgrade beyond that if needed. Second, the consultant and the computer facility had worked together closely in the past. Third, the computer facility had already installed most of the major pieces of software that would be required, such as the data base management system, the text processing software, and the budget management and financial applications software. Thus, not only was the software development task reasonable in scope but, since the program packages were already licensed to the computer facility, the college had no additional costs to pay beyond computer time, unless and until it acquired its own hardware. Fourth, the consultant chose to pursue a department-by-department, independent design approach, keeping the requirements of the whole college in mind but not getting bogged down in comprehensive designs right at the start. The consultant felt that it was important to establish some sense of progress and accomplishment early in the process and to maintain this sense throughout, even if some work had to be done over again later or at least fine-tuned on a second pass. The consultant disposed of rich tools in the development process and in part because college staff understood that the resulting systems were reasonably malleable over time; truly, this was software.

Implementation began on a sixteen-month schedule. Each department was addressed in turn. In each case, the department's existing manual and automated systems were examined in detail. From this examination, a functional specification of the systems to be implemented emerged. In a larger organization, this functional specification would have to be committed to paper; in the case of the college, so few people were involved that work could leapfrog immediately to the detailed design specification. In most cases, the design was thoroughly specified on paper to the satisfaction of all parties. This was probably the key to the success of the overall project. Since the work was done on a department-by-department basis, there was time to get each department head to sign off, indicating that the specifications for the department met the department's needs. Occasionally, time constraints or the unavailability of departmental personnel led to shortcuts. The college was fortunate that the consultant had spent enough time with the college and was sufficiently committed to the overall success of the project that most requirements were understood and accommodated even if there was not as much departmental involvement as desired.

In each case, the specifications that were developed served as permanent reference documentation for the system, which described the names and functional performance of each major program and report and the organization, content, and form of each type of data record in the system. The developer used some modern software development tools to make this important but tedious chore manageable.

Throughout the project, structured system design techniques were employed. Each system was designed from the top down, starting with broad descriptions of the performance required of the system and gradually narrowing down to specific program modules that fit together as required. Moreover, the design was tested and reviewed at each stage. Because departmental staff lacked computer sophistication, they were not involved in each iterative step of the design and implementation process. Instead, working together with the designer, they were required to specify the goals of each system; to accept, preferably in writing, the specification that the designer developed for each system before much implementation had begun; and to participate in training conducted by the designer when the system was ready for use.

Staff Support

Relatively early in the implementation process, the college hired a coordinator of information systems, whose responsibilities included acting as liaison between the software developer and the college, becoming fully knowledgeable about all implemented systems, acting as an in-house staff training and troubleshooting resource, and managing the overall project on a day-to-day basis on behalf of the chief administrator. Most important, the person chosen had excellent people skills and could therefore deal effectively with the problems that arose between department heads and between the developer and college staff. Indeed, his presence minimized the development of such problems. The ideal candidate for such a position comes to be recognized as an ally by all participants in the process.

Ultimately, the prescribed scope of work was completed close to schedule and within the budget specified. All departments had achieved most of what they wanted, although some departments did not achieve everything. Some desired functions were not addressed for one of several reasons, including low cost-effectiveness, poor understanding of the problem either by the developer or by departmental staff, or design complexity that would have lengthened the time schedule of the overall project. Everyone agreed that the functions could be addressed as part of a follow-up effort that would also smooth out rough edges left by the department-by-department approach.

Conclusions

What key lessons does this case study allow us to learn? First, while each department can achieve some useful results working on its own to create an automated information management system, an organizationwide approach, with support and involvement of top-level administrators, becomes critical as soon as several departments are using computers.

Second, the organizationwide approach typically means a centralized data base of information that each department can access and update simultaneously. Each department has access only to the data that it needs to do its work. The amount of redundant information required by departments—for example, student addresses and current class year—is best dealt with by an information structure that records such information only once. Updates by any authorized updating department are immediately available to all. Maintaining such information independently leads swiftly to information anarchy.

Third, any attempt to design a complete information management system in one fell swoop is likely to fail, because the information structures involved are very complex. It is better to choose a design and implementation approach that is rich enough to handle most of each department's announced needs in principle, then to deal with implementation of those needs one department at a time. Naturally, the developer must keep the collegewide picture firmly in mind during implementation. Further, the same developer or the same team of developers must be involved throughout the whole process, or anarchy can result. Finally, the approach produces usable systems early on in selected departments. This assures staff that progress is being made, and it attracts staff support for the overall implementation project.

Fourth, systems can be designed and implemented on short notice given the correct mix of resources. Modern programming languages and software development tools, such as the C language and the tools provided by the UNIX* and Idris** operating systems, substantially increase our ability to implement complex systems quickly, inexpensively, and correctly.

Fifth, the organizationwide approach does not imply that the institution must acquire a large and expensive on-site computing facility. Creative approaches, such as time-sharing on an existing computer with a compatible local organization, can be employed. Technologies exist to manage the related problems of information privacy and security.

Sixth, ample documentation is essential for continued operation and support of the system.

Seventh, recognition of the information management department as a collegewide resource for administrative departments, ideally by having it report directly to the chief administrative officer of the college, is important if services are to be provided equitably to all offices and if this equity is to be perceived as such. The nature of the person chosen to head that department is critical.

Eighth, preparation of a thorough needs analysis is an important first step that serves as a framework for the entire project. While the needs analysis should be considered a working document that can be revised during implementation, its importance as a mind setter cannot be underestimated.

Last, with proper administration and involvement by top management of the college, the risk involved in low-cost nontraditional approaches can be minimized, and the college can have a superior system.

* UNIX is a trademark of Bell Laboratories.
** Idris is a trademark of Whitesmiths, Ltd.

William H. Mayhew is president of The Village Systems Workshop, Inc., a firm in Natick, Massachusetts, that specializes in the specification, design, and development of computerized information management systems for nonprofit organizations. Before forming Village Systems, he directed the Computer Center at Boston's Children's Museum.

Presidents and chief financial officers must formulate plans for minimizing expense and maximizing revenues within the framework of the institution's objectives.

Providing Focus for Financial Management

Andrew J. Falender

An institution does not have to be in a crisis for a financial manager to improve its financial management, but it certainly helps. At the end of fiscal year 1975, the cumulative deficit at the New England Conservatory of Music was $744,000 (Figure 1). The annual operating budget was approximately $4 million. With a new management strategy and the dedication of trustees, faculty, and staff, we were able to reverse that financial trend during the next fiscal year. Since that time, we have produced seven consecutive years of operating surpluses. The cumulative deficit was completely eliminated in 1981, and at the end of 1982 the balance in the unrestricted current fund had reached $200,000. Moreover, the endowment fund increased from $4 million in 1975 to $12 million in 1983, providing further financial stability.

The basic formula for this financial turnabout was not new: Maximize revenue, and minimize expense. There are numerous routine and creative ways of accomplishing these two aims. The techniques are similar for both large and small institutions, and they are commonly known. The difficult part lies in developing a financial strategy that recognizes all the organization's primary goals and objectives, not just the financial ones.

New England Conservatory exists because it educates talented students of music. These students are attracted by the quality of the instruction. If that quality is sacrificed or seriously compromised, the best financial plan will not

A. J. Falender and J. C. Merson (Eds.). *Management Techniques for Small and Specialized Institutions.*
New Directions for Higher Education, no. 42. San Francisco: Jossey-Bass, June 1983.

Figure 1. Summary of Operations for 1973–1982, New England Conservatory of Music

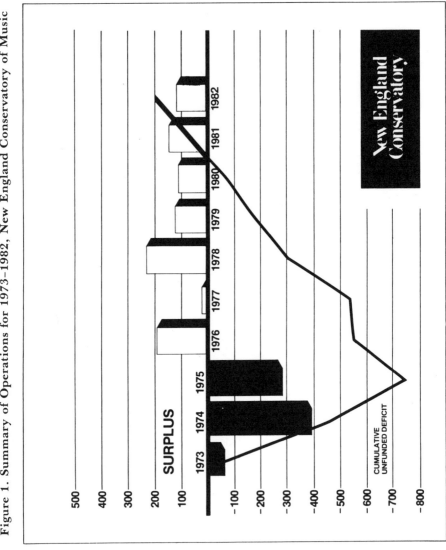

have a chance. This may seem obvious, but when deciding whether to cancel any of the twenty-three courses in which fewer than eight students have enrolled, it is essential to understand the nature of the institution. Will your financial decision significantly alter the actual or perceived quality of the school?

The goal of quality in instruction must be balanced with financial viability over the long run. One-time changes can look good, but institutions need improvements that help to change their norms and directions so benefits can be received year after year.

Implementing the Financial Plan

Before I discuss examples from the plan that we used at the Conservatory, I will discuss five strategies that ensure successful implementation. First, disseminate information and delegate authority to managers who can help. Dissemination of financial information and delegation of authority will enable the financial manager to take advantage of the tremendous potential for assistance from the institution's administrators. At New England Conservatory, we set up a budget formulation system that allowed managers to formulate their own department budgets within given guidelines. These guidelines came from an overall budgetary plan for the institution that produced either a balanced result or a surplus result to eliminate an unfunded deficit. Department managers are instructed to work within the guidelines and to propose whatever they think is necessary to meet their own department objectives. The objectives are submitted in writing. The department manager has an opportunity to petition for an increase over his allocation, but it is understood that strong justification is necessary for a favorable response. This participatory system encourages department heads to gain a feeling of ownership in the budget. At the same time, the guidelines protect the organization's overall financial and academic objectives.

Each administrative and faculty department head who is involved in the budget formulation process should understand the institution's overall financial structure and status. Department heads must understand how the budget structure has been developed and what assumptions have been used. To help department heads to place the guidelines for the current year in perspective, I share a five-year financial plan with them. Next, I meet with each department head in order to review his budget. I pull the department budgets together, work with the president to make decisions about requests that exceed the guidelines, and look at the revenue and expense totals. Most often, we find that the bottom line is not adequate, so we eliminate the programs in each department that have the lowest priority. Department heads are notified in writing of their final budget for the year. From this point, they have the authority to make all financial decisions themselves as long as they stay within the budget.

Second, build a control system that measures financial progress and communicates management's concern. When I arrived at the Conservatory, all accounting was done manually. Departments received their quarterly reports three to four months after the quarter ended. Some reports reflected expenditures that were six or seven months old. Without a great deal of effort, we implemented a computerized general ledger system. All programming, keypunching, and processing were handled by a service bureau. The new system has few frills, it is inexpensive, and it provides department and institution reports ten days after the end of the month. These reports compare, by expense category, actual expenditures with the budget developed by department heads. The reports help to identify problem areas quickly, so adjustments can be made. In addition, they allow me to report on year-to-date results and year-end projections for the school as a whole.

Showing department managers that top management cares about what they are doing should be a critical component of the control system. At the Conservatory, I try to write a comment on the monthly financial printout for each area. When significant problems are indicated, I write questions on the report and meet with the appropriate manager. In looking at any variance, positive or negative, a financial manager has to ask the right questions and understand how the reports influence department heads. In one situation, the department responsible for office supplies became more impressive every month. I assumed that the manager was buying items at low prices and motivating faculty and staff to make efficient use of supplies. Each month, I wrote a more glowing compliment. Then, in the spring I started to hear how difficult it was to obtain supplies. Department after department was going out and buying items on its own at full retail price. The manager of the supply center was saving money (with strong reinforcement from me), but no one could get supplies.

It helps to hold regular department head meetings. These meetings serve as a forum for giving recognition to managers who have done especially well in controlling expenses in their area, who have developed methods for efficiency, or who have generated additional revenues. I share the summary results for the whole school with department managers. It helps them to understand how their efforts influence the total organization. It also places peer pressure on individuals who are not doing as well as others.

If a manager thinks that no one is going to review his expenditures, he is much less likely to pay attention to them himself. At the Conservatory, we sign checks manually, so I am forced to review each one. While the controller has already cleared checks, it gives me an opportunity to catch anything that seems out of line and write a note to the department head. I strongly believe that the top people in an organization set the norms. If the president comes in late, leaves early, and misses days, it will be difficult to get other employees to pay attention to working hours. I have found that, if I eschew fancy furniture, extra telephone gadgets, and special stationery, faculty and staff are less likely to ask for such things.

Third, emphasize flexible areas with large dollar amounts. A manager's time is valuable, and it must be focused in the most promising directions. Some financial managers spend a great deal of time talking about the copying machine and how to control its use. The less flexible and smaller dollar areas should be influenced primarily by a general feeling of concern created in the institution. Controlling copying or supplies may not make much of a difference in the long run, but cash management often will. Another significant area for the New England Conservatory was energy savings through system improvements and temperature control. In both areas, the administrator has ultimate control, and there are tremendous possibilities for dollar savings.

The academic side of the institution requires a great deal of political sensitivity. I started by working within the existing structure. Looking at contracts, I found that many faculty members were not teaching a full load. Also, many classes were underenrolled. Working with the dean and the president, I identified changes that could be made without harming the academic program. For example, certain classes could be offered in alternative years. We saved for later years the very difficult questions of whether the course loads for faculty members were correct and whether we had appropriate classes and class size. Once a financial manager's credibility has been established, the administration will be in a better position to work with faculty to analyze the difficult issues.

Fourth, budget honestly but conservatively. Two primary and often conflicting institutional objectives are to improve quality on the one hand and the balance revenues with expenses on the other. A financial manager should ensure that the trade-off decisions involving these two conflicting objectives are made during the budget formulation process. If these decisions are not made then, they never will be. Once the year begins, there will be additional requests and overexpenditures. The only question is how many and how big.

Of course, there will always be pressure to respond to needs for items that could not have been predicted or that were forgotten during the budget formulation process. A financial manager will make allowances for these items. But, they also make it necessary to budget conservatively. Places where I try to make conservative estimates for budget purposes include interest rates, utility costs, endowment income, and total faculty costs. However, the financial manager must walk a fine line. If the financial manager gets too conservative, the president, trustees, and department heads will not be concerned about overspending. Also, policy makers will not take seriously the hard trade-off decisions that must be made before the budget can be brought into balance. Instead, they will assume that there is a cushion that can cover everything.

Financial savings are very difficult to obtain once the year has started. Faculty have been contracted, staff are in place, funds have been allocated to individual departments, program plans have been made in individual areas, and capital improvements are under way. Even minor cutbacks can have major implications. As the year goes on, some of the items that must be added are countered by favorable results. For example, last year at the Conservatory excess revenue from short-term cash investments helped to compensate for some necessary but unforeseen expenditures in teaching areas.

I do not budget conservatively or liberally in fund raising but try to be as realistic as possible. Before I arrived at the Conservatory, the budget was put together by listing all the projected expenses and subtracting the expected earned income. The difference was the annual fund-raising goal. In some years, this was a realistic amount, but in most years, it was not. However, if the estimate for fund raising is overly conservative, it reduces incentive for the fund raisers. Any conservatism should be included in other accounts.

Small institutions must be especially careful in the budgeting process. The Conservatory is so dependent on tuition income that a very small variation in enrollment can overwhelm all else that takes place. In the Conservatory's budget, an underenrollment of 1 percent — seven students — means that income drops by almost $50,000. This is equal to the total amount of leeway planned into the budget for any one year. The protection against such a drop in enrollment is a current fund surplus built up from past years. Then, a few years of lower enrollment can be weathered without bankruptcy.

Fifth, build and maintain credibility. Financial management does not need to involve a lot of wheeling and dealing or recruiting of political allies. However, trustees, faculty, and staff must understand what is going on, and they must see positive results for their efforts. An overall positive trend is the best way of building credibility for the financial manager.

An educational manager must be aware of and sensitive to the perspectives of the various constituencies within the organization. Nonprofit institutions are not very risk-oriented. New ideas and change must be instituted carefully and slowly. In presenting new ideas, the manager must make sure that he or she has basic credibility, that the votes are available on the issue, and if risk is involved that the gain is worth the cost.

For years, I thought that my most difficult problems would be over if the cumulative deficit could be eliminated. But, now that there is a surplus in the current fund, some people feel that careful budgeting and control are no longer necessary. Not all constituencies think of the long-term concerns. When I reported last year's surplus to the administrative department heads, they were not impressed. In fact, they wondered why the surplus should not be distributed immediately in the form of salary increases. Thus, when I reported the surplus to faculty department heads, I pointed out that, in relation to the Conservatory's total budget, the surplus was similar to a faculty member's having only $500 in savings for a rainy day. The analogy helped the group to understand the longer-term objective of financial security for the school. Once again, I was reminded that the challenge is long-term.

Minimizing Costs

As already noted, the financial plan has two basic components: Minimize costs, and maximize revenues. At the Conservatory, we try to minimize costs and maximize revenues by examining every facet of Conservatory operations on an ongoing basis. On the expense side, utility costs, contracting for services, personnel, and information processing have all been areas that needed improvement.

Utility costs were especially significant. Such savings are not one-time; they will recur year after year. In dollar terms, we would have to raise an additional $1.5 million in endowment in order to generate the benefit that we have achieved from utility savings alone. Most of the improvements required little technical expertise. For example, we found that water in the dormitory was being preheated all summer long, although the dormitory was closed. Exhaust fans were put on timers. System timers were installed to regulate heat with building use. We tightened the seals on windows and repaired the utility meter. The key to our success in this area was neither consultants nor a lot of expensive equipment but an intelligent individual who used common sense and cared about the institution.

We reduced expenses by contracting cleaning and security services. Use of the buildings during the regular academic year far exceeds summer use. When we staffed for the year, we had excess capacity during the slower months. We now avoid this waste, but we find that supervision of contractors is just as important as supervision of staff.

As we all know, faculty and staff costs are the largest expenditure in the budget of an institution of higher education. A simple review before the academic year begins will ensure that faculty are used to their full contract level. The next step requires a quantum leap. The issues of faculty loads, class size, and diversity of curriculum are policy issues that must fully involve the academic leadership of the school. While decisions on these issues are not under the control of the financial manager, he should make sure that he is involved. More important, he should make sure that the status quo is not taken for granted but instead that the issues are faced. A word of caution is in order: These are extremely sensitive areas for faculty, so the financial manager should make sure he does not lose his credibility here.

An understanding of which staff positions are of highest priority will help an institution to create a longer-term administrative plan. Implementing this plan may mean hiring additional staff in critical areas or reducing staff in other departments. For a small institution, it is usually difficult to reduce staff. Most positions cover several functions, and each function is necessary for the operation of the school. But, as individuals leave, their position can be analyzed to ensure that the marginal benefit to the institution is worth the cost. Of course, staff should not remain on the payroll if they are not competent. Firing unproductive individuals is not pleasant, but it is critical to maintaining the financial good health of the institution and the expectations that employees have about the organization.

My last point about minimizing expenses concerns the flow of information within the organization. When I arrived at the Conservatory, I could not understand the difference between the record keeping in the dean's office and the record keeping in the registrar's office. The administrative heads of the two department defended the systems as necessary. A year later, we hired a new registrar and found that the processes in the two offices were totally duplicative. In fact, the information did not flow at all. Seven years ago, four full-time staff members were employed in the registrar's office to serve 600 students. Now, we have 700 students and one and one-half full-time staff.

Maximizing Revenue

Revenue decisions can be challenging and difficult, but they also allow us to be creative. I will discuss eight areas: tuition levels, enrollment size, cash investment, endowment, financial aid, auxiliary services, extension services, and real estate investments.

The pricing and quantity decisions are the most difficult. My working assumption is that New England Conservatory is trying to sell a product on the high end of the quality continuum. This means that the demand curve is relatively inelastic. In other words, students are not as price-sensitive as they might be if the quality of the product were lower. Following this reasoning, we have instituted a very aggressive policy on tuition increases each year. At the same time, we have increased scholarship allocations by greater than proportional amounts to ensure that talented students who lack the necessary financial resources are not excluded.

The size of the school poses a difficult problem, and solving it requires a policy decision that must involve the board of trustees as well as the administration. It is tempting to boost the financial results by adding a few more students. Unfortunately, if ten students are added in one year, it is even more tempting to add another ten in the next. In order to improve the financial situation at the Conservatory, we increased the student body by almost 10 percent. However, before we did, we looked at the number of applications that we received to make sure that we would not have to go lower than we wished in musical quality. We also examined our facilities to see whether there was room in which to expand. In each case, there were significant sacrifices. When you admit an additional 10 percent you are admitting students who previously would have been judged to have less potential than the students whom you admitted. In addition, the space constraints become more difficult. The decision has to be made whether the sacrifices are balanced by the benefits.

If enrollment is increased in order to generate additional revenue, the financial manager must make sure that expenses do not also increase. Almost without exception, administrative departments and faculty requested more staff to respond to the larger student body, even if the department's activities were unrelated to the increase in volume. Unless the line is held in these situations, no ground can be gained. There are no hard-and-fast rules. For the Conservatory, additional staff and faculty were added in some cases but only to ensure that the administration ran smoothly and that the quality of instruction remained high.

The importance of cash management has already been noted. When I arrived at the Conservatory, the yearly income from investment of idle cash balances was $5,000. By maintaining a near-zero balance in the checking account and by keeping the maximum balance in money market instruments, the Conservatory earned $220,000 last year. Even considering the increase in interest rates and cash balances, the point is still valid. Board members with investment expertise and relevant bank officials can give advice on money market instruments. The main responsibility of the financial manager is to make sure that all cash balances are fully invested.

The investment of endowment funds is also critical. Careful planning can make it congruent with the institution's other financial objectives. Short-term and long-term investment strategies have very different implications. When the Conservatory was in a financial crunch in 1975, we decided to shift our emphasis from stocks to bonds. That decision significantly increased our cash flow, but it also compelled us to sacrifice gain in the longer term. College administrators and trustees should not accept any policy as given. Instead, they must continually evaluate their investment policy to make sure that it is consistent with other short-term and long-term objectives.

A similar trade-off is involved in the relative emphasis on contributions to the endowment fund and contributions to the annual campaign. Obviously, the best strategy for the long run is to build the endowment, but current expenditure needs can curtail efforts on behalf of that objective until a more stable financial plateau has been reached. A significant amount of my time each year — as much as 25 percent — goes into fund raising, both endowment and annual. Corporations, foundations, and in many cases individuals are at least as concerned about the institution's finances as they are about substantive issues. People seem to be more skeptical of the financial management of a small institution. Therefore, they need to be convinced that their money will be well spent. This is especially true if the institution has had severe financial difficulties in the recent past.

The subject of student financial aid receives extensive coverage in all the specialized publications reaching higher education institutions. In spite of this, the president or chief financial officer of a small institution should make sure that the institution is maximizing federal and state government grants. I came to the Conservatory from the Department of Health, Education, and Welfare, so I was surprised to learn that the school received only $12,000 from federal student aid programs and that it did not participate in the College Work Study Program at all. I asked the financial aid officer why this was the case and she replied that the funds that the school would receive were not worth the trouble of filling out the necessary forms. This year, the Conservatory received more than $200,000 from that program, even despite the recent cutbacks. From National Direct Student Loans (NDSL), Supplemental Educational Opportunity Grants (SEOG), Basic Educational Opportunity Grants (BEOG), and College Work Study, we will receive a total of $420,000 for the current year. Financial aid officers are very important in small institutions. They must be capable, they must be familiar with federal and state funding sources, and they must work hand-in-hand with the directors of admissions to ensure that enrollment goals are met. A review of this area is well worth the financial manager's time.

As a general rule, dormitory and food service operations should break even on a direct cost basis. This is only a guideline, since the fees charged for the dormitory and food service need to be seen as a part of the overall pricing structure. If a potential freshman sees the room and board costs as excessive in relation to those of another school that he or she is considering, all the efforts to make sure that tuition is priced correctly have been wasted. A simple yearly survey of room and board fees charged by competitors has been very helpful to us in reaching a final decision.

Through its Extension Division, the Conservatory offers nondegree instruction, both lessons and class programs, to children and adults. Seven years ago, the Extension Division lost approximately $20,000 on a direct cost basis. This year, the division should exceed expenses and contribute approximately $60,000 to general Conservatory overhead. In addition, we have started a summer school, which in the long run should both contribute to general overhead and provide employment opportunities for faculty during the summer months. In both cases, we pursued aggressive pricing strategies and changed our philosophy from one that such activities always lose money to one that the operation should be run as much like a business as possible. As in any good business, the quality of the product is critical, but that does not prevent consideration of financial concerns. Here, too, the key to effective operations is the individual in charge: someone who understands the necessity of good business practices yet will not compromise musical quality.

The last revenue area that I want to mention involves our recent purchase of an old office building across the street. The Conservatory needed practice rooms for its students even before the 10 percent enrollment increase. Purchase of this building has given us more practice space. In the long run, this acquisition will not increase overhead. Indeed, it will be a net revenue producer. We plan on using about 25 percent of the space. The remainder will be leased. The projections for the first year, which involve substantial renovations and less than full occupancy, show almost a break-even position. The money to purchase the building came from the endowment fund. It may be the best investment decision ever made for that fund.

Conclusions

The overriding theme is that financial moves must be compatible with the institution's other goals and objectives. But, producing a high-quality product is not an excuse for inefficiency or lack of creativity in administrative operations. The financial manager must keep in mind the implications of a decision for the long run. While short-run successes can make an administrator look good for a while, they do not constitute the best contribution to the institution.

To help ensure that the institution's financial plan is implemented successfully, five strategies should be considered: Disseminate information and delegate authority to managers who can help. Build a control system that measures financial progress and communicates management's concern. Emphasize flexible areas with large dollar amounts. Budget honestly but conservatively. Build and maintain credibility.

Finally, financial management depends on leadership. Individuals who have intelligence and common sense and who understand the purpose of the institution are the most critical components of success.

All institutions of higher education, no matter how large or how small, are going to face difficult challenges during the rest of this decade: There are fewer students in the admissions pool, costs continue to rise, and fund raising is becoming ever more competitive. Placing priority on financial management will not remove any of these problems, but it will help an institution to survive them.

Andrew J. Falender is chief executive officer of the New England Conservatory of Music.

For the college president, associations can be servant or master:
They can enhance educational good husbandry, or they can sap
educational purpose.

Small Colleges and Associations

Frank A. Tredinnick, Jr.

The sheer number of associations is intimidating. Choosing the right associations is a challenge for the cost-conscious president. Few guidelines are universally useful. It is safe to say, however, that it is wise to beware of those who would sell memberships rather than deliver service.

Service is the only justification for the existence of an association. The relevance of that service to the needs of the institution is the first basis for judgment about the wisdom of membership. The effectiveness with which the service is delivered and the cost of delivery are equally important. Information on costs is usually easily available. The tendency of many associations to base dues on enrollment means that the small college enjoys the same benefits as the large institution at lower cost. Information on the effectiveness with which the association delivers service is best obtained from peers. Phone calls to presidents who are not members as well as to those who are can provide quick and accurate insights into effectiveness.

It is more difficult to make a judgment about the relevance of an association's activities to the individual college, because the pre-conditions of good judgment are rigorous institutional and presidential self-knowledge. That is, the president must know what he wants an association to provide as well as what the association does provide. Membership in a handful of associations — the tendentiously named voluntary accrediting agencies, for example — is a necessity, not an option. Such memberships are convenient gateways to federal funds, and the president's needs are not germane. A judicious selection

A. J. Falender and J. C. Merson (Eds.). *Management Techniques for Small and Specialized Institutions.*
New Directions for Higher Education, no. 42. San Francisco: Jossey-Bass, June 1983.

of memberships that are truly optional can provide the skillful president with surrogates or substitutes for staff, a direct or indirect means of providing or saving money, status, a forum for discussion and learning, timely information, a means of making useful acquaintances, and a resource enabling the institution to do what it cannot do itself.

Associations dealing with national and state governments are particularly useful in providing surrogates or substitutes for staff. Many large institutions have a government relations staff—often one of substantial size—but the small institution may not have enough money to hire and sustain even a single employee in this field. The need to know how to get government funds and how to ward off government threats is important for both types of institution. Association membership could very well be the most cost-effective answer for the small institution.

The state and regional associations of colleges formed to raise money from business and industry provide an obvious example of direct assistance in providing money to members. Indirect assistance can result from an association's efforts on behalf of increased financial aid. An association can produce savings directly by offering reduced rates on services and specialized purchases; indirectly by passing on information about new techniques. Sharing knowledge on new energy-saving practices is a familiar example of indirect savings.

Except in the case of a few associations with closed membership, status is not conferred by membership in educational associations. Nevertheless, status lies in the eye of the beholder, and if a particular constituency—alumni, for example—is impressed by the company that an institution keeps, then membership can be a very real consideration. Prominent display of membership certificates in the halls of academe is an indication that for many institutions there is at least the perception that association membership enhances status.

There is a myth earnestly fostered by those who file large expense accounts that the great truths of academic administration are to be found only late at night in some of the nation's tonier watering places, usually in the wake of an association meeting. This is not so, but association activities do provide opportunities for comparing notes with peers, for getting to know others—often leaders in the field—and for identifying issues. These opportunities can be important for newcomers. The formal programs of worthwhile associations are usually timely and relevant, but the interchanges prior to a meeting or during breaks are often equally rewarding.

For many, the most important consideration in decisions about association membership involves their role as an information source. Accurate information, skillfully and rapidly provided, is a basic and invaluable management tool. Well-run associations can be identified by their communications programs. They select the important information and make it easily accessible. They do not cry wolf. They avoid information overload. If they publish a newsletter, it contains news and not filler. They differentiate between the urgent and the important, and they respond to the needs of their constituency as the constituency perceives them.

An association can provide an opportunity not simply for meeting other members, important as that may be, but of getting to know resource people outside its membership. Staff people of associations can be and should be reasonably available. Speakers at association meetings can become unexpectedly helpful friends. Officers of neighboring institutions are sometimes more readily available at association meetings than on their own campus.

Finally, even the most assured institution finds tasks that can better be accomplished in the company of others. Associations exist to provide a means of bringing institutions together to perform such tasks for agreed upon common purposes. There is no point in having an association do what a member institution can do more effectively and more economically.

A few associations may offer all these attributes. In my experience, if an association offers at least four and if they match the needs of the president and the institution, the possibility of membership should be investigated. It is imperative to remember, however, that an association can possess all seven attributes and still be inappropriate for the individual institution. This is particularly true of the larger national associations, and it is here that cost and effectiveness judgments must be rigorously applied.

The problem is not hypothetical. For example, because resources are limited, scores of college presidents each year must choose a single membership from among such organizations as the American Council on Education, the National Association of Independent Colleges and Universities, and the Council of Independent Colleges and Universities. Each of these organizations can fairly be said to perform most of the functions just outlined. Each is well-staffed. Each communicates well with its constituency. Assuming that any decision is not going to be reached on the basis of price alone, then the testing question is, Precisely what would the institution miss if it were not a member of this association? The question has to be put in the negative to force the ruthless thinking that should characterize decisions on association membership. There always seem to be an infinite number of reasons to pay dues for what one would gain, but the true reason to be for dues paying lies in what one would lose.

In the best of all possible worlds, an institution would belong to all three associations. For many, perhaps for most, this is not possible. Accordingly, a tough-minded decision must be made based on the loss that nonmembership would mean. What can tip the balance in such considerations is special services that may only be evident on inquiry. Some associations lend files on a variety of professional concerns, thereby making available the best examples of successful institutional experiences. Some provide workshops on pertinent subjects at a variety of locations that make it easy for members to attend. Some provide data services completely customized to the needs of the individual institution. Many provide current research reports and state-of-the-art monographs. Finally, some provide placement services of varying degrees of formality. These are a few examples of potentially valuable services that membership can make available.

Presidents need to be careful about using dues as the sole indication of the cost of membership, and a last-minute comparison of the real cost of membership with the dues cost can be the determinant in considerations about which associations to join and which to forget. The real cost takes the cost of dues as a basis and then adds the cost of attending meetings, including transportation costs, hotel and meal costs, and registration fees. Registration fees are especially important, because they have escalated in recent years to a point where the conscientious president will give some serious thought to the question of whether an annual meeting is really worth the money. Association executives are given to justifying high registration and service fees for meetings on the basis not of increased service to the membership, but of increased costs to the association. While those who complain may be pilloried as cheap, they may be admired as solvent in the long run.

Most associations will prove to be only as good as the level of expectation established by members. Membership in an association is not a passive role. Small-college presidents should recognize that the benefits of association membership are enhanced by participation, and if an association is worth joining, it is also worth spending time participating in its affairs. There are some association activities that presidents will not wish to delegate, but in most associations the institution's interests can be represented by someone other than the president. Whoever represents the institution should not hesitate to make suggestions and to ask questions, but at the same time this individual should have an accurate sense of where suggesting leaves off and carping begins.

Suggestions made by directors and officers of associations obviously carry the most weight. Ideally, an institution should not join an association unless it is willing to supply the appropriate individual for a post as an officer or director at some time in the future. There is no mystery about how one becomes an officer or director: One demonstrates that one is interested, that one has something to offer, and that one is willing to work with others. Often, considerations of geography and institutional type are taken into account in creating boards, but manifest ability and obvious enthusiasm transcend other considerations with great frequency.

Governance of associations takes many forms. The distinction that anyone making serious inquiry into the worth of association membership must make is whether policy decisions are made by members or by staff. In a good association, staff will array options, members will make decisions, and staff will implement these decisions. Few effective associations allow staff to set policy as well as to implement it. In cases where staff are given completely free rein, it is usually because the task that the association professes to address is one that is distasteful to presidents. Political work comes to mind as an example.

The governing board of an association should meet often enough to accomplish the job at hand. There is a fine distinction between the number of meetings necesssary to make sure that the job gets done and the number of meetings held simply to hold a meeting. Too many educators still believe that they have accomplished something by holding a meeting. Good associations make sure that the work of their governing board is communicated to members on a timely basis. Small associations sometimes consider the possibility of open meetings of the governing board. Careful attention to minutes and other publications can provide a president not only with a sense of what is going on in the field but also with a sense of what is not going on. This sense can suggest topics for future meetings.

Too many associations are run by cliques or are controlled by one or two dominant members. There is potential for good in such a situation—more operational effectiveness is often advanced as an argument—but more often than not tightly held control means that an association is inhospitable to new ideas. The most debilitating arrangements involve both members and staff and result in extremely low turnover in board and committee assignments. Such a situation, of course, is not known on college campuses, and hence it is unexpected in associations.

The staff of associations are the individuals with whom the small-college president will talk most frequently, and a friendly, knowledgeable association staff member can often become a great asset to a member institution that makes an effort to get acquainted. However, individuals who work for associations are not always the elite of the profession. Moreover, association executives tend to stay at their jobs too long. Unlike those employed on college campuses, their activities are not subjected to oversight, and the result is substantial inertia. Here again, members have an obligation to make sure that they have the kind of staff that they need. Too often, members do not take advantage of the assets that association staff members have. Never hesitate to ask a question simply because it may not appear to be immediately germane to the staff member's responsibility. An amazing amount of information accretes to association executives, and one of their great values should be that if they do not know the answer, they know where to find it.

Once they are started, associations seem to go on forever. They can be organized from time to time, but they rarely self-destruct. This state of affairs results from the fact that, once an institution makes the decision to join an association, it rarely reassesses its position. However, as budgets become increasingly tight, the small college can no longer afford the luxury of unexamined membership. Increasingly, tough-minded cost-benefit analyses of membership will become the order of the day. More institutions may follow the lead of one exceptionally well-run college whose senior management team each year rank-orders the value of all of its association memberships. The association that finishes last is dropped. The same group also acts on all proposals for new membership, but it does not necessarily add an association simply because another association has been dropped.

In discussions of this sort, someone will usually ask whether the major benefits of membership may not be available even if the institution discontinues its support. In a surprising number of cases, nonmembers reap the same benefits as members. For example, an association that suggests and helps to bring about changes in the tax code benefits members and nonmembers alike. In such cases, the decision on membership will reflect institutional morality perhaps more than it does the institutional balance sheet.

Tighter budgets also make the financial affairs of associations a matter of increasing interest to members. Good associations help to make financial evaluation easier by providing annual independently audited financial statements. These statements can provide insight into the association's attitude toward itself: Is it a means or an end? Large reserves and an asset base heavy in non-liquid assets, such as real estate, are two signals that the association is more concerned about its own interests than about the interests of members.

In addition to the direct effect that tighter budgets will have on an association's well-being, there is an indirect effect that clouds the future of many associations. Associations are basically a device for sharing based on mutual trust. As the number of students decreases and prices rise, competition may come to dominate the everyday life of the small college. Too often, as competition increases, trust decays, and this can undermine the informing principle of most associations. Nevertheless, attractive opportunities still remain for the conscientious president to make association memberships work productively for the benefit of the institution.

Frank A. Tredinnick, Jr., is executive vice-president of the Association of Independent Colleges and Universities in Massachusetts.

Building an effective board requires attention to trustees' roles and reponsibilities, selection of new trustees, board organization, and criteria for measuring trustees' performance.

The Board of Trustees

Robert L. Qualls

The aim of this chapter is to help trustees of institutions to clarify and perhaps to reformulate their own definition of both the obligation and the opportunity of trusteeship. In most institutions, the performance of institutional management falls far short of what is possible with the available resources. As a rule, trustees have not asserted themselves in the role required both by their legal obligations and by the socioethical burden of public trust that they carry (Greenleaf, 1974). The overall performance of each institution can be raised by a governing board that organizes to do so. Thus, this discussion will focus on the how-tos of building an effective trustee group. The effective board must not only be goal-directed, it must also develop a structure that will allow its members to be a functioning part of the institution's leadership.

The Role of Trustees

The bylaws of the institution usually specify the actions that board members themselves must take and the actions that they may delegate to administrative officers. Above and beyond these specific actions, trustees have five major functions in the management of institutions (Greenleaf, 1974): They participate in formulating the broad policy guidelines within which the institution will operate. They appoint the executive officers. They assess the performance of the institution. They enhance the institution's image. Finally, they ensure financial viability.

A. J. Falender and J. C. Merson (Eds.). *Management Techniques for Small and Specialized Institutions.*
New Directions for Higher Education, no. 42. San Francisco: Jossey-Bass, June 1983.

The role of trustees in setting the policy within which the institution will operate should include guidelines for all the parties involved. However, the established goals are the trustees' own goals. In setting these goals, trustees need to address the question raised by Drucker (1964): What business are we in, and what are we trying to accomplish? The institution needs to state clearly where it wants to go, whom it wants to serve, and how it expects those whom it serves directly (as well as society at large) to benefit from that service. Unless these goals are clearly stated, an institution cannot reach the desired level of performance.

Two of the most important jobs of trustees are to select the chief executive officer and to evaluate his performance at regular intervals. Trustees are also responsible for the overall design of the top administrative structure, which encompasses the duties and appointment of those recommended to these offices by the president. Board members should never simply rubber-stamp administrative recommendations on these matters. In addition, trustees must assess the work of the total institution and ensure its financial health. These responsibilities include not only the approval and monitoring of the budget but the management of endowments and their own personal involvement in annual fund solicitations and capital campaigns as well.

The Selection of Trustees

Several considerations are involved in the selection of trustees for the institution. These factors include the total number of trustees, the lengths of their terms and the level of their responsibility, the extent to which the institution's service area and the trustees' residence must tie together, the necessary and the desirable qualities of trustees, the identification and cultivation of prospects, and the president's role in trustee selection.

The number of trustees and the length of their terms of appointment are extremely important to a well-functioning board. Obviously, there is no so-called right number of trustees, and the number can range between as few as seven and as many as sixty-seven or more, depending on what proves workable. A board that is too big can be hard to mold into an effective team. In the case of large boards, much of the work is best done by committees; as a result, the full board will meet less often. A board that is too small cannot represent all the institution's various constituencies. This can cause individual trustees to be overworked or to lose interest quickly. To remedy the situation, a number of institutions have created advisory type boards, which have worked well when they have been properly structured and when their functions have been well defined.

Once the number of trustees has been determined, it is important to develop a specific term of appointment for each new trustee. For example, if the number of trustees happens to be thirty-three and if trustees are appointed for a three-year term, then new appointments can be arranged so that eleven of the thirty-three are rotated off the board each year. Under this arrangement, the board has an opportunity to reappoint trustees who are doing a good job and to replace the less productive trustees with new ones.

Some boards have found it desirable to limit the term of appointment to two consecutive terms of three years each, after which the trustee must automatically leave the board for one year in order to become eligible for reappointment. Obviously, there are some good points and some bad points to this system. While it allows the board to replace poor performers, it can also allow the board to lose the services of good trustees. In institutions where this system is used, it has been found that good trustees develop other interests during their year off the board and do not want to return when invited. Consideration should also be made for different classifications of trustees, such as life members, honorary members, and past members. In most cases, only regular members have the priviledge of voting.

In most trustee groups, there is an ongoing effort to identify potential members. The president of the institution often has more exposure to the various constituencies of the institution than any other one person, so he or she should be able to identify and cultivate potential trustees. Individual board members are also excellent sources. Some institutions have boards of visitors or advisory boards that provide good training grounds for future trustees.

Finally, while it is difficult to pinpoint all the essential qualifications for trusteeship, the late president of Brown University, Henry Wriston, said that he looked for three basic ingredients: work, wisdom, and wealth. President Wriston preferred a prospective trustee to possess all three characteristics, but he would consider an individual who possessed only two.

Board Organization

Several factors, such as the number of trustees, the frequency of meetings, and the willingness of individual trustees to assume positions of leadership, influence board organization. Obviously, there is no perfect committee system, but if they are properly structured, six committees can be very helpful to a well-functioning board (Ingram and Associates, 1980): an executive committee, a nominating committee, a finance committee, a development committee, an academic affairs committee, and a student affairs committee. Nonboard members, such as students and faculty leaders, should serve on the last three.

Executive Committee. In practice, the executive committee has most of the powers of the board when it is not in session, and it exercises these powers in case of emergency. Generally, the chairman of the board serves as chairman of the executive committee. The membership normally includes committee chairmen and the board officers. While the executive committee can be extremely important to the work of the institution, care must be taken to ensure that it does not act on matters that are the primary responsibility of other committees. It is a good practice for the full board to review and approve the minutes of the executive committee. The chief executive should provide staff support and serve as an ex officio member of this committee.

Nominating Committee. Although the nominating committee is often neglected, it is extremely important to the work of the board. Aside from developing a set of criteria for board membership, this committee has the responsibility of identifying, cultivating, and enlisting new trustees. It is also the duty of this committee to develop the necessary orientation for new members and to deal with trustees who have become ineffective. The chief executive officer should staff this committee.

Finance Committee. The finance committee is responsible for working with the president and the chief financial officer in the areas of budgeting, financial planning, and endowment and investment management. In cases where the investment function is extensive, the board can consider creating a separate investment committee or a subcommittee of the finance committee. It is extremely important for the finance committee not to shirk its oversight role, and it is imperative for it to work with the administration in developing an effective monitoring system. This committee, or a subcommittee of it, is usually responsible for the audit function. The chief financial officer serves as staff support for this committee.

Development Committee. While the development committee is primarily responsible for fund raising, it should be understood that it does not have the exclusive responsibility for raising funds. The board as a whole has a duty to see that the funds necessary to support the approved budget are available. The director of development or the director of college relations performs the role of staff support.

Academic Affairs Committee. The academic affairs committee should be involved with such items as student recruitment, admission requirements, the academic program, budgets, honorary degrees, faculty personnel policies, and tenure appointments. The committee's agenda should also include strategic planning issues that affect the academic program and the faculty (Merson and Qualls, 1979). This committee should be staffed by the chief academic officer. It offers the best opportunity of any board committee for building a friendly and cooperative relationship with faculty. One or two faculty and student leaders should be ex officio members.

Student Affairs Committee. The student affairs committee plays a key leadership role by arranging opportunities for trustees to meet with students in various campus activities. The committee should also be involved in the quality of student services on campus, including student government activities and programs. Finally, it should serve as an effective instrument for resolving conflict when established administrative channels have been exhausted. The staff resource person to this committee should be the dean of student services.

Although much of the work of an effective board is done by committees, it is important for the full board to meet at least two or three times a year.

At the full board meetings, it is not only possible to review and assess the work of the various committees, but each trustee can enter into a dialogue with fellow trustees on key issues affecting the institution's future.

Measuring Trustee Effectiveness

Effective trusteeship requires an ongoing commitment to introspective self-appraisal. A board can evaluate its own policies, practices, and organizational structure in a number of different ways. Obviously, there is no single best way, but three approaches have proved helpful: ad hoc meetings, questionnaires, and consultants.

If ad hoc meetings are used to measure board effectiveness, it is important for these sessions to be held at times other than those of the regular meetings. Ad hoc meetings can be used to conduct in-depth discussions of a single problem area, or they can simply be used to discuss issues that fall into the good of the order category.

If they are properly used, questionnaires are probably the best way of assessing board performance through self-study. Considerable effort is required to design the questions and to administer and analyze the questionnaires. Not everyone is willing to give the time and thought necessary to answer the questions. This is especially true when the questions involve personal perceptions of problems.

From time to time, the board may find that an outside point of view is needed. This outside view can be provided by a well-qualified consultant. A consultant may also be the best way of minimizing tensions and finding solutions that are acceptable to board members when strong differences of opinion are known to exist.

There is no set rule on how often a board should study its own performance, and there are no accepted standards against which the board can judge itself. A number of institutions have found that a meeting built around an annual retreat is a good way to review and evaluate board performance, since it combines a conference on issues with a social event in which spouses can be included. The mixing of work and pleasure goes a long way to develop the overall team approach to trusteeship.

Since each institution has different obligations, structures, and functions, no single set of criteria will allow every board to assess its performance. Ingram and Associates (1980) have listed five criteria: the mission of the institution, including strategic planning issues; financial resources and the physical plant; the educational program; board relationships with the president, faculty, students, alumni, and other constituent groups; and board memberships.

The rationale for self-evaluation studies by the board of trustees involves the issue of accountability. Trustees must hold themselves accountable not only to the institution on whose board they serve—the administration, faculty, students, and alumni — but to the public as well. Thus, a commitment to trusteeship requires an ongoing commitment to self-appraisal.

Conclusion

The central thrust of this chapter is that, to build an effective board, all the members must be involved in decision making. To accomplish full participation requires the board to develop a clear and agreed upon role for itself, a role that is not only goal-directed but that also has the structure necessary to permit its members to be a functioning part of the institution's leadership. It is equally important for the board to appraise the effectiveness of its work on an ongoing basis. When all is said and done, the final responsibility falls on the board.

References

Drucker, P. F. *Managing for Results*. New York: Harper & Row, 1964.
Greenleaf, R. K. *Trustees as Servants*. Cambridge, Mass:. Center for Applied Studies, 1974.
Ingram, R. T., and Associates. *Handbook of College and University Trusteeship: A Practical Guide for Trustees, Chief Executives, and Other Leaders Responsible for Developing Effective Governing Boards*. San Francisco: Jossey-Bass, 1980.
Merson, J. C., and Qualls, R. L. *Strategic Planning for Colleges and Universities: A System Approach to Planning and Resource Allocation*. San Antonio: Trinity University Press, 1979.

Robert L. Qualls is executive vice-president of Worthen Bank and Trust Company. Under Governor Bill Clinton, he served as Arkansas's chief financial officer. For five years, he was president of the College of the Ozarks, where he is currently a trustee.

Index

A

Addison-Wesley, 9
Administrators: hiring of, by president, 19–20, 56–57; as interpreters to president, 61; senior, organizing, 59–64; as spokesmen, 61
Admissions: analysis of, 33–39; current students as recruiters for, 38–39, 46; and enrollment plan, 35–37; and feeder schools, 38; and financial management, 80; and foreign students, 34; and image building, 45–46; impact of enrollment decline on, 34–35; and inquiry pool, 38; institutional research for, 37; market research information for, 36–37; materials and staff for, 37–38; plan for, 37–39; responsibility for, 35; and student shortage, 33–34
Allen, C., 2, 33–39
Alumni: fund raising from, 26, 29; and image building, 44–45
American Council on Education (ACE), 36, 87
Apple IIe, 10
Ashby, R., 2, 41–47
Association of American Colleges, 51
Association of Governing Boards of Universities and Colleges, 51
Associations: activities of, 86; analysis of, 85–90; costs of membership in, 88; financial statements from, 90; governance of, 88–89; and governmental relations, 86; as information source, 86–87; and mutual trust, 90; regional, 86; relevance of, 85–86; resource people in, 87; responsibilities of membership in, 00; services of, 85, 87–88; staff of, 89
Axelrod, N. R., 15, 23

B

Basic Educational Opportunity Grants (BEOG), 81
Bell Laboratories, 71n
Blake, W., 18

Blyn, M. R., 13, 17, 18, 22
Bolman, F. D., 50, 57, 58
Boyan, D. R., 34, 39

C

Change, and presidential leadership, 18
Cleveland, H., 18–19, 22
College Work Study Program, 81
Compaq Portable, 10
Computers: analysis of, for information systems, 65–71; background on, 65–66; conclusions on, 70–71; needs analysis for, 67; personal, in planning, 8, 9–10; proposals for, evaluating, 67–68; staff support for, 70; system design and implementation for, 68–69; time sharing on, 68
Constituent relationships, presidential concerns about, 13
Cooperative Institutional Research Program, 36
Corcoran, R. J., 2, 25–31
Corporations, fund raising from, 26, 29–30
Council of Independent Colleges and Universities, 87
Cowley, W. H., 16, 22
Corriculum, presidential concerns about, 12
Cyert, R. M., 17, 23

D

Dean of the college, presidential hiring of, 19–20
Dec VT-100, 10
Department heads, and financial management, 75, 76
Donors: cultivation of, 29–30; identification of, 28
Drucker, P. F., 19, 23, 92, 96

E

Educational Testing Service (ETS), 36–37
Enrollment plan, and admissions, 35–37

Evaluation: in planning, 5, 6, 10; of presidents, 20–21; of trustee effectiveness, 95–96

F

Faculty: and image building, 43–44; presidential concerns about, 12; and presidential leadership, 16–17
Falender, A. J., 1–3, 73–83
Farnham, L. J., 55, 58
Federal government, as funding source, 14, 81–82
Financial management: analysis of, 73–83; and auxiliary services, 82; budgeting in, 77–78; and cash management, 81; conclusions on, 82–83; control system for, 76; and cost minimizing, 78–80; credibility in, 78; and department heads, 75, 76; of endowment, 81; and enrollment size, 80; and extension programs, 82; of faculty and staff costs, 79; flexibility with large dollar amounts in, 77; implementation of, 75–78; information dissemination in, 75; and information processing, 79–80; and real estate, 82; and revenue maximizing, 80–82; and services contracting, 79; of student aid, 81–82; and tuitions, 80; of utility costs, 79
Financial planning, 5, 7–8, 10
Fisk, E. C., 20, 23
Foundations: fund raising from, 26, 30; and image building, 46–47
Fouts, D. E., 54, 58
Francis, N. C., 14, 23
Frantzreb, A. C., 14, 23
Fund raising: analysis of, 25–31; case statement for, 25–27; elements in, 25; feasibility study for, 27; and image building, 46–47; leadership for, 27–28; presidential responsibility for, 13–14; and prospect market, 28–30; self-study for, 26–27; suggestions on, 30; and trustees, 25, 26, 27

G

Greenleaf, R. K., 18, 23, 91, 96

H

Hampshire College, management structure at, 59–64

Hesburgh, T., 22, 23
Hodgkinson, H. L., 19, 23

I

IBM-PC, 10
Idris, 71
Image, public: and admissions, 45–46; and alumnae, 44–45; analysis of, 51–47; background on, 41–42; for campus and community, 43–44; conclusions on, 47; defining, 42–43; and faculty, 43–44; and fund raising, 46–47; and mission, 42, 46; president's responsibility for, 43, 44, 45, 46, 47
Information systems, computer-supported, 65–71
Ingram, R. T., 93, 95, 96

K

Kauffman, J. E., 51, 55, 58
Korda, M., 18, 23

L

Leadership: for fund raising, 27–28; management different from, 17; presidential responsibility for, 16–19
Lotus Development Corporation, 9
Lotus 1-2-3, 9–10
Lutheran Church in America, 51

M

Maccoby, M., 18, 23
McConnell, W. R., 33, 36, 39
McKenna, S., 43
Management: and associations, 85–90; of computer-supported information systems, 65–71; financial, 73–83; of fund raising, 25–31; of image, 41–47; leadership different than, 17; need for, 1; of planning, 5–10; by president, 11–23; of recruitment and admissions, 33–39; of selecting administrators, 49–58; of staffing, 59–64; by trustees, 91–96
Market research, information sources on, 36–37
Mayhew, L. B., 14, 19, 23
Mayhew, W. H., 2, 65–71
Merson, J. C., 1–3, 5–10, 20, 23, 94, 96
Micro-DSS/Finance, 9–10
Microsoft, 9

Mission: and image, 42, 46; and presidential leadership, 16; and strategic planning, 6; and trustee role, 91
Multiplan, 9-10

N

Nason, J. W., 15, 23, 49, 51, 57, 58
National Association of Independent Colleges and Universities, 87
National Direct Student Loans (NDSL), 81
Ness, F. W., 18, 23
New England Conservatory of Music, financial management at, 73-83
Newman, J. H., 18

P

Parents, fund raising from, 29
Pattillo, M. J., 57, 58
Pine Manor College, image building at, 41-47
Planning: analysis of, 5-10; computers for, 8, 9-10; cycle for, 5-8; evaluation in, 5, 6, 10; financial, 5, 7-8, 10; monthly meetings for, 5, 8; organizing process of, 8-9; resource allocation in, 5, 6-7; strategic, 5, 6, 10; timetable for, 8-9; and trustees, 6, 7
Presidential search: analysis of, 49-58; and announcement of vacancy, 53; background on, 49-50; committee for, 50-51; conducting, 52-56; confidentiality in, 52; consultants for, 51; cost of, 51; information types needed in, 52-53; interviews in, 54-56; organizing, 50-52; and reluctant candidates, 54; screening in, 54; and selection, 56; timetable for, 51, 53
Presidential Search Consultation Service, 51, 57
Presidents: administrators hired by, 19-20, 56-57; and admissions, 35, 36; analysis of role of, 11-23; concerns of, as candidates, 11-13; evaluation of, 20-21; and faculty, 12, 16-17; and fund raising, 13-14; and image, 43, 44, 45, 46, 47; and leadership, 16-19; responsibilities of, 13-20; rewards for, 21-22; search for, 49-58; trustee concerns of, 11-12; trustee relationships with, 14-16

Q

Qualls, R. L., 3, 20, 23, 91-96

R

Recruitment. *See* Admissions
Resources: allocation of, 5, 6-7; presidential concerns about, 12
Richardson, R. C., Jr., 20, 23

S

Simmons, A., 2, 59-64
Smith, G. T., 14, 16, 23
Staffing: analysis of, 59-64; and areas needing oversight, 60; factors essential in, 63-64; and flexibility, 62; issues in, 59-60; of middle management positions, 62; and personnel policy, 63; presidential concerns about, 12-13; and reporting relationships, 60-61; and training young people, 63
Strategic planning, 5, 6, 10
Students: financial aid for, 81-82; foreign, and admissions, 34; presidential concerns about, 12; recruitment and admission of, 33-39; as recruiters, 38-39, 46; shortage of, 33-35
Supplemental Educational Opportunity Grants (SEOG), 81

T

Tredinnick, F. A., Jr., 3, 85-90
Trustees, board of: academic affairs committee of, 94; analysis of, 91-96; development committee of, 94; evaluation of effectiveness of, 95-96; evaluation of president by, 20-21; executive committee of, 93-94; finance committee of, 94; and fund raising, 25, 26, 27; nominating committee of, 94; organization of, 93-95; and planning, 6, 7; presidential concerns about, 11-12; presidential relationships with, 14-16; responsibilities of, 15; role of, 91-92; and search for president, 50-52, 56; selection of, 92-93; student affairs committee of 94-95

U

Unglaube, J. M., 2, 49-58
UNIX, 71

V

Vice-presidents, search for, 56–57

W

Weaver, S. R., 55, 58
Wenrich, J. W., 16, 23
Wesleyan College, and student recruit-
ers, 38

West, D. C., 2, 11–23
Western Interstate Commission on
Higher Education (WICHE), 33, 36
Whitesmiths, 71n
Wriston, H., 93

Z

Zoerner, C. E., Jr., 13, 17, 18, 22